When it comes to kids, Kohl's cares. We actively support kids' health and education initiatives in communities nationwide. With over a decade of dedication and hundreds of millions of dollars raised, we aim to give kids a happier, healthier future.

Throughout the year, Kohl's sells kid-friendly cause merchandise, with 100 percent of the net profit donated to support kids' health and education initiatives in communities nationwide. Since 2000, more than $208 million has been raised through our Kohl's Cares® cause merchandise program.

For more information on Kohl's community giving, visit Kohls.com/Cares.

Kids' Treats

Publications International, Ltd.

Louis Weber, CEO
Publications International, Ltd.
7373 North Cicero Avenue
Lincolnwood, IL 60712

Pictured on the front cover: Banana Split Ice Cream Sandwiches *(page 82).*
Pictured on the jacket flap: Building Blocks *(page 118).*
Pictured on the back cover *(left to right):* Crazy Colors Cupcakes *(page 236)* and
Mini Dizzy Dogs *(page 8).*

ISBN-13: 978-1-4508-6884-6
ISBN-10: 1-4508-6884-3

Library of Congress Control Number: 2012954907

Manufactured in China.

8 7 6 5 4 3 2 1

Microwave Cooking: Microwave ovens vary in wattage. Use the cooking times as guidelines
and check for doneness before adding more time.

Publications International, Ltd.

Contents

Reinvented Classics

Mac and Cheese Mini Cups

   3 tablespoons butter, divided
   2 tablespoons all-purpose flour
   1 cup milk
   1 teaspoon salt
½ teaspoon black pepper
   1 cup (4 ounces) shredded sharp Cheddar cheese
   1 cup (4 ounces) shredded Muenster cheese
½ pound uncooked elbow macaroni, cooked and drained
⅓ cup toasted bread crumbs

1. Preheat oven to 400°F. Melt 1 tablespoon butter in small saucepan over low heat. Grease 36 mini (1¾-inch) muffin cups with melted butter.

2. Melt remaining 2 tablespoons butter in large saucepan over medium heat. Whisk in flour; cook 2 minutes. Add milk, salt and pepper; cook and stir 3 minutes or until mixture is thickened. Remove from heat; stir in cheeses. Fold in macaroni.

3. Divide macaroni and cheese among prepared muffin cups. Top with toasted bread crumbs.

4. Bake 20 to 25 minutes or until golden brown. Cool 10 minutes in pans; remove carefully using sharp knife.

Makes 36 appetizers

Meat Loaf Cupcakes

  3 medium potatoes, peeled and chopped
1½ pounds 90% lean ground beef
  ½ cup finely chopped onion
  ⅓ cup old-fashioned oats
  1 egg
  2 tablespoons chopped fresh rosemary
  ½ cup milk
  2 tablespoons butter
  1 teaspoon salt
    Black pepper
  ¼ cup snipped chives

1. Preheat oven to 350°F. Place potatoes in medium saucepan; cover with water. Bring to a boil; cook 25 to 30 minutes or until potatoes are fork-tender.

2. Meanwhile, combine beef, onion, oats, egg and rosemary in large bowl; mix well. Divide mixture among 10 standard (2½-inch) muffin cups. Bake 25 minutes or until cooked through (145°F).

3. Beat potatoes, milk, butter, salt and pepper in large bowl with electric mixer at medium speed 3 minutes or until smooth. Place potato mixture in large piping bag fitted with large star tip.

4. Remove meat loaf cupcakes to serving platter. Pipe mashed potatoes on top for frosting. Sprinkle with chives.   *Makes 10 servings*

Meat Loaf Cupcakes

Mini Dizzy Dogs

½ sheet (8-ounce can) refrigerated crescent roll dough
20 mini hot dogs or smoked sausages
    Ketchup and mustard

1. Preheat oven to 375°F. Line baking sheet with parchment paper.

2. Slice dough rectangle lengthwise into 20 (¼-inch) strips. Coil 1 dough strip around 1 hot dog. Place onto prepared baking sheet. Repeat with remaining dough strips and hot dogs.

3. Bake 10 to 12 minutes or until light golden brown. Serve with ketchup and mustard for dipping.

Makes 20 appetizers

Sloppy Joe Sliders

12 ounces 90% lean ground beef
 1 can (about 14 ounces) stewed tomatoes with Mexican seasonings
½ cup frozen mixed vegetables, thawed
½ cup chopped green bell pepper
 3 tablespoons ketchup
 2 teaspoons Worcestershire sauce
 1 teaspoon ground cumin
 1 teaspoon cider vinegar
24 mini whole wheat rolls, split and warmed

1. Brown ground beef in large nonstick skillet over medium-high heat, stirring to break up meat; drain fat.

2. Add tomatoes, mixed vegetables, bell pepper, ketchup, Worcestershire, cumin and vinegar; bring to a boil. Reduce heat; cover and simmer 15 minutes or until peppers are tender and mixture has thickened. Break up large pieces of tomato.

3. To serve, spoon 2 tablespoons meat mixture onto each bun.

Makes 24 mini sandwiches

Mini Dizzy Dogs

BLT Biscuits

2 cups all-purpose flour
2 teaspoons sugar
2 teaspoons baking powder
1 teaspoon black pepper
½ teaspoon baking soda
½ teaspoon salt
⅓ cup cold butter, cut into small pieces
1 cup (4 ounces) shredded Cheddar cheese
¾ cup buttermilk
1 package (16 ounces) bacon slices, cooked
1 small head romaine lettuce
4 plum tomatoes
½ cup mayonnaise

1. Preheat oven to 425°F. Line baking sheets with parchment paper.

2. Combine flour, sugar, baking powder, pepper, baking soda and salt in large bowl. Cut in butter with pastry blender or two knives until mixture resembles coarse crumbs. Stir in cheese and buttermilk just until mixture forms dough.

3. Turn dough out onto lightly floured surface; knead gently several times. Pat into 8×6-inch rectangle (about ¾ inch thick). Cut dough into 24 squares with sharp knife; place on prepared baking sheets. Bake 10 to 12 minutes or until golden brown. Cool slightly on wire rack.

4. Cut each bacon slice into 3 pieces. Tear lettuce into small pieces to fit on biscuits. Cut tomatoes into ¼-inch slices.

5. Split biscuits; spread each half lightly with mayonnaise. Layer each biscuit with 2 slices bacon, lettuce and 1 slice tomato. *Makes 24 mini sandwiches*

Turkey Club Biscuits: Prepare BLT Biscuits as directed above, adding deli sliced turkey and avocado slices.

BLT Biscuits

Micro Mini Stuffed Potatoes

    1 pound small new red potatoes
 ¼ cup sour cream
    2 tablespoons butter, softened
 ½ teaspoon minced garlic
 ¼ cup milk
 ½ cup (2 ounces) shredded sharp Cheddar cheese
 ½ teaspoon salt
 ¼ teaspoon black pepper
 ¼ cup finely chopped green onions (optional)

Microwave Directions

1. Pierce potatoes with fork in several places. Microwave potatoes on HIGH 5 to 6 minutes or until tender. Let stand 5 minutes; cut in half lengthwise. Scoop out pulp from potatoes and place in medium bowl. Set potato shells aside.

2. Beat potato pulp with electric mixer at low speed 30 seconds. Add sour cream, butter and garlic; beat until well blended. Gradually add milk, beating until smooth. Add cheese, salt and pepper; beat until blended.

3. Fill each potato shell with equal amounts of potato mixture. Microwave on HIGH 1 to 2 minutes or until cheese melts. Garnish with green onions.   *Makes 4 servings*

Micro Mini Stuffed Potatoes

Croque Monsieur Bites

8 thin slices firm sandwich bread
4 slices Swiss cheese, halved (about 4 ounces)
4 slices smoked ham (about 4 ounces)
   Dash grated nutmeg
2 tablespoons butter, melted

1. Cut crusts from bread. Place 4 slices bread on work surface. Layer each with half slice cheese, 1 slice ham and remaining half slice cheese; sprinkle with nutmeg. Top with remaining 4 slices bread. Brush outside of sandwiches with melted butter.

2. Cook sandwiches in large skillet over medium heat 2 to 3 minutes per side or until golden brown and cheese is melted. Cut into quarters.

Makes 16 pieces

Tip

These sandwiches can be prepared ahead of time and reheated for an easy party appetizer. Leave sandwiches whole after cooking and refrigerate until ready to serve. Cut into quarters and place on foil-lined baking sheet; bake in preheated 350°F oven about 8 minutes or until sandwiches are heated through and cheese is melted.

Croque Monsieur Bites

Soft Pretzels

1¼ cups milk
4 to 4½ cups all-purpose flour, divided
¼ cup sugar
1 package active dry yeast
1 teaspoon baking powder
1 teaspoon garlic salt
½ cup (1 stick) unsalted butter, melted
2 tablespoons baking soda
Coarse salt, sesame seeds or poppy seeds

1. Heat milk in small saucepan over low heat to 105° to 115°F.

2. Beat 3 cups flour, sugar, yeast, baking powder and garlic salt in large bowl with dough hook of electric mixer at low speed. Add milk and butter; beat vigorously 2 minutes. Add remaining flour, ¼ cup at a time, until dough begins to pull away from side of bowl.

3. Turn dough out onto lightly floured surface; flatten slightly. Knead 10 minutes or until smooth and elastic, adding flour if necessary to prevent sticking.

4. Shape dough into ball. Place in large, lightly oiled bowl; turn dough to grease top. Cover with towel; let rise in warm place about 30 minutes.

5. Divide dough into 18 equal pieces. Roll each piece into 22-inch-long rope on lightly oiled surface. Form each rope into U shape. About 2 inches from each end, cross dough. Fold loose ends down to rounded part of U; press ends to seal. Turn pretzels over so that ends are on bottom and reshape if necessary. Cover with towel; let rest 20 minutes.

6. Preheat oven to 400°F. Grease baking sheets or line with parchment paper. Fill large Dutch oven three-fourths full with water. Bring to a boil over high heat. Add baking soda. Carefully drop pretzels, 3 at a time, into boiling water for 10 seconds. Remove with slotted spoon. Place on prepared baking sheets. Sprinkle with coarse salt, sesame seeds or poppy seeds.

7. Bake 15 minutes or until golden brown. Place on wire racks; cool completely.

Makes 18 large pretzels

Soft Pretzels

Grilled Cheese Kabobs

8 thick slices whole wheat bread
3 thick slices sharp Cheddar cheese
3 thick slices Monterey Jack or Colby Jack cheese
2 tablespoons butter, melted

1. Cut each slice of bread into 1-inch squares. Cut each slice of cheese into 1-inch squares. Make small sandwiches with 1 square of bread and 1 square of each type of cheese. Top with second square of bread.

2. Place sandwiches on the end of short wooden skewers. Brush 4 sides of sandwiches with melted butter.

3. Heat nonstick grill pan over medium-high heat. Grill sandwich kabobs 30 seconds on each of 4 sides or until golden and cheese is slightly melted.   *Makes 12 servings*

Tuna Schooners

1 can (6 ounces) tuna packed in water, drained and flaked
½ cup finely chopped apple
¼ cup shredded carrot
⅓ cup ranch salad dressing
2 English muffins, split and lightly toasted
8 triangular-shaped tortilla chips

1. Combine tuna, apple and carrot in medium bowl. Add salad dressing; mix well.

2. Spread one fourth of tuna mixture on top of each English muffin half.

3. Press 2 chips firmly into tuna mixture to form sails.   *Makes 4 servings*

Grilled Cheese Kabobs

Italian Chicken Nuggets

¼ cup all-purpose flour
1 egg, lightly beaten
1 cup toasted bread crumbs
½ cup grated Parmesan cheese
2 teaspoons dried Italian seasoning
Salt and black pepper
3 boneless skinless chicken breasts, cut into 1-inch pieces
Olive oil cooking spray
Warm pasta sauce

1. Preheat oven to 400°F. Line baking sheet with parchment paper.

2. Place flour in shallow bowl. Place egg in second shallow bowl. Combine bread crumbs, cheese, Italian seasoning, salt and pepper in third shallow bowl.

3. Dip each piece of chicken into flour, then in egg, then roll in bread crumb mixture. Place on prepared baking sheet. Spray chicken with cooking spray.

4. Bake for 25 minutes or until nuggets are browned and cooked through. Serve with warm pasta sauce for dipping.

Makes 4 servings

Tip

Need a break from chicken? Cubed pork tenderloin would be an outstanding substitute!

Italian Chicken Nuggets

Game's On

Tiny Shrimp Tacos with Peach Salsa

1 peach, peeled and finely diced
2 tablespoons finely chopped red onion
1 small jalapeño pepper,* finely chopped (optional)
Juice of 1 lime
1 tablespoon chopped fresh parsley or cilantro
1 clove garlic, minced
½ teaspoon salt
8 (6-inch) flour tortillas
1 tablespoon vegetable oil
1 pound medium raw shrimp, peeled, deveined and cut into small pieces
2 teaspoons chili powder

*Jalapeño peppers can sting and irritate the skin, so wear rubber gloves when handling peppers and do not touch your eyes.

1. Combine peach, onion, jalapeño, if desired, lime juice, parsley, garlic and salt in medium nonreactive bowl. Set aside.

2. Preheat oven to 400°F. Cut out 24 (2½-inch) tortilla rounds using cookie cutter or sharp knife. Discard scraps. Place tortilla rounds over handle of wooden spoon; secure with toothpicks. Bake 5 minutes; repeat with remaining tortilla rounds.

3. Heat oil in large nonstick skillet over medium-high heat. Add shrimp and chili powder; cook and stir 3 minutes or until shrimp are pink and opaque.

4. Place a few shrimp pieces in each taco shell; top each taco with peach salsa.

Makes 24 tacos

Buffalo Wedges

3 pounds Yukon Gold potatoes
2 tablespoons hot pepper sauce
2 tablespoons butter, melted
2 teaspoons smoked or sweet paprika
Blue cheese dressing

1. Preheat oven to 400°F. Spray baking sheet with nonstick cooking spray. Slice potatoes into 4 or 6 wedges, depending on size of potato.

2. Combine hot pepper sauce, butter and paprika in large bowl. Add potato wedges; toss to coat well. Place wedges in single layer on prepared baking sheet.

3. Bake 20 minutes. Flip potatoes; bake 20 minutes or until light golden brown and crisp. Serve with blue cheese dressing. *Makes 4 servings*

Poblano Pepper Kabobs

1 large poblano pepper*
4 ounces smoked turkey breast, cut into 8 cubes
4 ounces pepper jack cheese, cut into 8 cubes
¼ cup salsa (optional)

Poblano peppers can sting and irritate the skin, so wear rubber gloves when handling peppers and do not touch your eyes.

1. Preheat oven to 400°F. Soak 4 wooden skewers in warm water 20 minutes to prevent burning.

2. Meanwhile, fill medium saucepan half full with water; bring to a boil over medium-high heat. Add pepper; cook for 1 minute. Drain. Core, seed and cut pepper into 12 bite-size pieces. Thread 1 piece pepper, 1 piece turkey and 1 piece cheese onto each skewer. Repeat, ending with pepper.

3. Place kabobs on baking sheet. Bake 3 minutes or until cheese starts to melt. Remove immediately. Serve with salsa, if desired. *Makes 4 servings*

Buffalo Wedges

Super Bowl Snack Mix

½ cup packed brown sugar
1 teaspoon chili powder
½ teaspoon salt
½ teaspoon curry powder
½ teaspoon five-spice powder
1½ cups raw almonds
1 cup dried cherries
1 cup shelled raw pistachio nuts
1 egg white

1. Preheat oven to 250°F.

2. Combine brown sugar, chili powder, salt, curry powder and five-spice powder in medium bowl; stir well. Add almonds, cherries and pistachios; mix well.

3. Whisk egg white in large bowl until frothy. Add almond mixture; toss to combine.

4. Spread mixture evenly onto nonstick baking sheet. Bake 35 to 40 minutes, stirring occasionally. Let mixture cool 30 minutes or until coating is firm. Break into small chunks. Store mix in airtight container.

Makes 14 servings

Super Bowl Snack Mix

Baked Pork Buns

1 tablespoon vegetable oil
2 cups coarsely chopped bok choy
1 small onion or large shallot, thinly sliced
1 container (18 ounces) refrigerated shredded barbecue pork
2 containers (10 ounces each) refrigerated buttermilk biscuit dough

1. Preheat oven to 350°F. Grease baking sheets.

2. Heat oil in large skillet over medium-high heat. Add bok choy and onion; cook and stir 8 to 10 minutes or until vegetables are tender. Remove from heat; stir in barbecue pork.

3. Lightly dust work surface with flour. Remove biscuits from containers and separate into individual biscuits. Split 1 biscuit in half crosswise to create two thin biscuits. Roll each biscuit half into 5-inch circle.

4. Spoon heaping tablespoon pork mixture onto one side of circle. Fold dough over filling to form half circle; press edges to seal. Arrange buns on prepared baking sheet. Repeat with remaining biscuits and filling. Bake 12 to 15 minutes or until golden brown.   *Makes 20 buns*

Baked Pork Buns

Chili Cheese Mini Dogs

2 teaspoons chili powder
½ sheet (8 ounce can) refrigerated crescent roll dough
5 slices sharp Cheddar cheese
20 mini hot dogs

1. Preheat oven to 375°F. Line baking sheet with parchment paper.

2. Sprinkle 1 teaspoon chili powder evenly over each side of dough. Cut dough into 20 squares.

3. Cut each cheese slice into 4 squares. Press 1 cheese square onto 1 dough square. Place 1 hot dog in center; bring up sides of dough to secure hot dog. Place onto prepared baking sheet. Repeat with remaining cheese, dough and hot dogs.

4. Bake 12 minutes or until dough is golden brown.

Makes 20 servings

Chili Cheese Mini Dogs

Zucchinidillas

Nonstick cooking spray
1 tablespoon vegetable oil
1 zucchini, thinly sliced
$\frac{1}{2}$ cup thinly sliced red onion
$\frac{2}{3}$ cup green salsa, divided
$\frac{1}{2}$ cup (2 ounces) shredded Cheddar cheese
$\frac{1}{2}$ cup (2 ounces) shredded Monterey jack cheese
6 (6-inch) flour tortillas, divided
$\frac{1}{2}$ cup sour cream

1. Preheat oven to 400°F. Line baking sheet with foil. Spray with cooking spray.

2. Heat oil in medium skillet over medium-high heat. Add zucchini and onion; cook and stir 5 minutes or until vegetables are softened. Stir in $\frac{1}{3}$ cup salsa; remove from heat. Stir in cheeses.

3. Place 3 tortillas on baking sheet. Divide zucchini mixture among tortillas. Top with remaining 3 tortillas. Spray top tortillas with cooking spray. Bake 8 minutes or until cheese is melted and tortillas are crisp.

4. Combine sour cream and remaining $\frac{1}{3}$ cup salsa in small bowl. Cut quesadillas into wedges; serve with sour cream mixture.   *Makes 4 to 6 servings*

Zucchinidillas

Quirky Bites

Porky Pinwheels

1 sheet frozen puff pastry, thawed
1 egg white, beaten
8 slices bacon, crisp-cooked and finely chopped
2 tablespoons packed brown sugar
¼ teaspoon ground red pepper

1. Place pastry onto piece of parchment paper. Brush surface with egg white.

2. Combine bacon, brown sugar and ground red pepper in small bowl. Sprinkle evenly over top; press lightly to adhere. Roll pastry jelly-roll style from long end. Wrap in parchment paper. Refrigerate 30 minutes.

3. Preheat oven to 400°F. Line baking sheet with parchment paper. Slice pastry into ½-inch-thick slices. Place 1 inch apart on prepared baking sheet.

4. Bake 10 minutes or until light golden brown. Remove to wire racks; cool completely.

Makes 24 pinwheels

Green Eggs

½ cup chopped green bell pepper
⅓ cup chopped parsley
3 tablespoons dill pickle relish
2 egg whites
1 teaspoon dried basil
1 teaspoon dried oregano
½ teaspoon salt
½ teaspoon black pepper
1 pound ground turkey
¼ cup uncooked oats
1 tablespoon olive oil
Hot Tomato Dipping Sauce (recipe follows)

1. Place bell pepper, parsley, relish, egg whites, basil, oregano, salt and black pepper in food processor or blender. Pulse until bell pepper is finely minced. Add turkey and oats; pulse 2 or 3 times or until just mixed. Chill mixture 15 minutes.

2. Preheat oven to 325°F. Shape mixture by tablespoonfuls into egg-shaped meatballs. Heat olive oil in nonstick skillet over medium heat. Brown meatballs on all sides. Place on nonstick baking sheet. Bake 10 to 15 minutes or until cooked through. Serve warm with dipping sauce.

Makes 16 meatballs

Hot Tomato Dipping Sauce

½ cup chopped tomato
½ cup vegetable broth or water
2 tablespoons tomato paste
1 teaspoon Italian seasoning
Hot pepper sauce (optional)

Combine tomato, broth, tomato paste and seasoning in small saucepan. Cook over low heat until just simmering. Season with hot pepper sauce, if desired. Serve with meatballs.

Green Eggs

Great Zukes Pizza Bites

  1 medium zucchini
  3 tablespoons pizza sauce
  2 tablespoons tomato paste
  $\frac{1}{4}$ teaspoon dried oregano
  $\frac{3}{4}$ cup (3 ounces) shredded mozzarella cheese
  $\frac{1}{4}$ cup shredded Parmesan cheese
  8 slices pitted black olives
  8 slices pepperoni

1. Preheat broiler; set rack 4 inches from heat.

2. Trim off and discard ends of zucchini. Cut zucchini into 16 ($\frac{1}{4}$-inch-thick) diagonal slices. Place on nonstick baking sheet.

3. Combine pizza sauce, tomato paste and oregano in small bowl; mix well. Spread scant teaspoon sauce over each zucchini slice. Combine cheeses in small bowl. Top each zucchini slice with 1 tablespoon cheese mixture, pressing down into sauce. Place 1 olive slice on each of 8 pizza bites. Place 1 folded pepperoni slice on each remaining pizza bite.

4. Broil 3 minutes or until cheese is melted. Serve immediately.   *Makes 8 servings*

Great Zukes Pizza Bites

Guacamole Cones

6 (6-inch) flour tortillas
1 tablespoon vegetable oil
1 teaspoon chili powder
2 ripe avocados
1½ tablespoons fresh lime juice
1 tablespoon finely chopped green onion
¼ teaspoon salt
¼ teaspoon black pepper
Dash hot pepper sauce (optional)
2 to 3 plum tomatoes, chopped

1. Preheat oven to 350°F. Line baking sheet with parchment paper.

2. Cut tortillas in half. Roll each tortilla half into cone shape; secure with toothpick. Brush outside of each cone with oil; sprinkle lightly with chili powder. Place on prepared baking sheet.

3. Bake 9 minutes or until cones are lightly browned. Turn cones upside down; bake about 5 minutes or until golden brown on all sides. Cool cones 1 minute; remove toothpicks and cool completely.

4. Cut avocados in half; remove and discard pits. Scoop avocado pulp from skins and place in medium bowl; mash with fork. Stir in lime juice, green onion, salt, pepper and hot pepper sauce, if desired, until blended.

5. Fill bottom of each tortilla cone with about 1 tablespoon chopped tomato; top with small scoop of guacamole and additional chopped tomatoes. Serve immediately.

Makes 12 cones

Guacamole Cones

Bavarian Pretzel Sandwiches

4 frozen soft pretzels, thawed or Soft Pretzels (page 16)
1 tablespoon German mustard
2 teaspoons mayonnaise
8 slices Black Forest ham
4 slices Gouda cheese
1 tablespoon water
Coarse pretzel salt or kosher salt

1. Preheat oven to 350°F. Line baking sheet with parchment paper.

2. Carefully slice each pretzel in half crosswise using serrated knife. Combine mustard and mayonnaise in small bowl. Spread mustard mixture onto bottom halves of pretzels. Top with 2 slices ham, 1 slice cheese and top halves of pretzels.

3. Place sandwiches on prepared baking sheet. Brush tops of sandwiches with water; sprinkle with salt. Bake 8 minutes or until cheese is melted.   *Makes 4 sandwiches*

Bavarian Pretzel Sandwich

Salsa Hummus Dip

1 container (8 ounces) prepared hummus
½ cup mayonnaise
2 to 3 tablespoons salsa
1 tablespoon minced green onion
Pita chips and/or vegetables

1. Combine hummus, mayonnaise, salsa and green onion in medium bowl. Refrigerate until ready to serve.

2. Serve with pita chips.

Makes about 6 servings

Prep Time: 5 minutes

Tip

Use this flavorful dip to liven up sandwiches or wraps.

Salsa Hummus Dip

Roasted Edamame

2 teaspoons vegetable oil
2 teaspoons honey
½ teaspoon kosher salt
1 package (10 ounces) shelled edamame, thawed if frozen
Additional salt (optional)

1. Preheat oven to 375°F.

2. Combine oil, honey and salt in large bowl; mix well. Add edamame; toss to coat. Spread on baking sheet in single layer.

3. Bake 12 to 15 minutes or until golden brown, stirring once. Immediately remove from baking sheet to large bowl; season with additional salt, if desired. Cool completely before serving. Store in airtight container.

Makes 4 to 6 servings

Roasted Edamame

Polenta Cheese Bites

 3 cups water
 1 cup corn grits or cornmeal
½ teaspoon salt
¼ teaspoon chili powder
 1 tablespoon butter
¼ cup minced onion or shallot
 2 teaspoons minced jalapeño pepper* (optional)
½ cup (2 ounces) shredded sharp Cheddar cheese or fontina cheese

Jalapeño peppers can sting and irritate the skin, so wear rubber gloves when handling peppers and do not touch your eyes.

1. Grease 8-inch square baking pan. Bring water to a boil in large nonstick saucepan over high heat. Slowly add grits, stirring constantly. Reduce heat to low; cook and stir until grits are tender and water is absorbed. Stir in salt and chili powder.

2. Melt butter in small saucepan over medium-high heat. Add onion and jalapeño, if desired; cook and stir 3 to 5 minutes or until tender. Stir into grits; mix well. Spread in prepared pan. Let stand 1 hour or until cool and firm.

3. Preheat broiler. Cut polenta into 16 squares. Arrange squares on nonstick baking sheet; sprinkle with cheese. Broil 4 inches from heat 5 minutes or until cheese is melted and slightly browned. Remove immediately. Cut squares in half. Serve warm or at room temperature. (Polenta will firm as it cools.)   *Makes 32 appetizers*

Tip: For spicier flavor, add ⅛ to ¼ teaspoon red pepper flakes to the onion-jalapeño mixture.

Polenta Cheese Bites

Kiddie Creations

Snake Snacks

2 small ripe bananas
1 tablespoon fresh lemon juice
10 to 12 medium strawberries, hulled
2 small strawberries
Poppy seeds (optional)

1. Cut bananas crosswise into ¼-inch slices. Place in medium bowl; toss gently with lemon juice to prevent bananas from turning brown.

2. Leave 2 medium strawberries whole; cut remaining medium strawberries crosswise into ¼-inch slices.

3. Place whole strawberries on serving plates for heads; alternate banana and strawberry slices behind heads to form snakes. Arrange small strawberries at end of snakes.

4. Cut 4 small pieces of banana for eyes; arrange on snake heads. Place poppy seed in center of each eye, if desired.   *Makes 2 servings*

Tip: Try to choose strawberries that are about the same diameter as the banana so all the fruit slices that make up the snake will be close to the same width.

Friendly Face Pizzas

  3 whole wheat English muffins, split in half
¾ cup pasta sauce
¾ cup (3 ounces) shredded Italian cheese blend
  Assorted vegetables

1. Preheat oven to 400°F. Place English muffin halves on baking sheet.

2. Spread pasta sauce onto muffins. Sprinkle with cheese. Create silly faces on top of cheese with desired vegetables.

3. Bake 8 to 10 minutes or until cheese is melted.   *Makes 6 servings*

Great Green Veggie Wedgies

½ cup whipped cream cheese
 2 (8- to 10-inch) spinach tortillas
¼ cup apricot or peach fruit spread
½ cup coarsely chopped fresh baby spinach
¼ cup grated carrot

1. Evenly spread cream cheese over one side of each tortilla.

2. Spread fruit spread over cream cheese on one tortilla. Sprinkle spinach and carrot over fruit spread.

3. Place the second tortilla, cheese side down, on top of the spinach and carrot. Lightly press tortillas together.

4. Cut the tortilla sandwich into 8 wedges.   *Makes 2 servings*

Friendly Face Pizzas

Breakfast Mice

 2 hard-cooked eggs, peeled and halved lengthwise
 2 teaspoons mayonnaise
 ¼ teaspoon salt
 2 radishes, thinly sliced and root ends reserved
 8 raisins or currants
 1 ounce Cheddar cheese, shredded or cubed
   Spinach or lettuce leaves (optional)

1. Gently scoop egg yolks into small bowl. Mash yolks, mayonnaise and salt until smooth. Spoon yolk mixture back into egg halves. Place 2 halves, cut side down, on each serving plate.

2. Cut two tiny slits near the narrow end of each egg half; position 2 radish slices on each half for ears. Use the root end of each radish to form tails. Push raisins into each egg half to form eyes.

3. Place small pile of cheese in front of each mouse. Garnish with spinach.

Makes 2 servings

Breakfast Mice

Creepy Cobwebs

    4 to 5 cups vegetable oil, divided
    1 cup dry pancake mix
¾ cup plus 2 tablespoons milk
    1 egg, beaten
½ cup powdered sugar
    1 teaspoon ground cinnamon
½ teaspoon chili powder
    Dipping Sauce (recipe follows)

1. Pour 1 inch of oil into large deep skillet; heat to 350°F.

2. Combine pancake mix, milk, egg and 1 tablespoon oil in medium bowl. *Do not overmix.* Place 2 tablespoons batter into funnel or squeeze bottle; swirl into hot oil to form cobwebs. Cook until bubbles form. Gently turn using tongs and slotted spatula; cook 1 minute or until browned. Drain on paper towels.

3. Repeat with remaining batter. If necessary, add more oil to maintain 1-inch depth and heat oil to 350°F between batches.

4. Meanwhile, mix powdered sugar, cinnamon and chili powder in small bowl. Sprinkle over cobwebs. Serve cobwebs warm with Dipping Sauce.   *Makes 10 to 12 servings*

Dipping Sauce

    1 cup maple syrup
    1 jalapeño pepper,* cored, seeded and minced

Jalapeño peppers can sting and irritate the skin, so wear rubber gloves when handling peppers and do not touch your eyes.

Combine syrup and jalapeño in small saucepan. Simmer 5 minutes or until syrup is heated through. Pour into heatproof bowl.   *Makes 1 cup*

Creepy Cobwebs

Bird-wich

Mayonnaise or mustard
3 round slices deli meat
1 bottom half round sandwich bun
1 round sandwich bun, split
3 round slices cheese
2 leaves romaine lettuce
1 black olive
2 peas
Parsley sprigs (optional)

1. Layer mayonnaise and 2 slices deli meat on 1 bottom bun. Top with second bottom bun, mayonnaise, remaining slice deli meat and 1 slice cheese. Cut circle out of front end of top bun angling towards center of bun with round cutter. Spread mayonnaise on cut side of top bun and place on top of cheese.

2. For wings, insert 2 lettuce leaves between cheese and top bun on opposite sides of back of sandwich. For beak, cut 1 slice cheese in half. Loosely roll 1 half; roll other half slightly tighter and insert into looser half. Insert beak into hole in bun, cut sides in.

3. For eyes, cut olive in half crosswise. Attach to bun above beak with dabs of mayonnaise. Insert peas into holes in olives. For feet, cut 2 triangles out of remaining slice cheese. Cut 2 small V shapes out of short side of each triangle. Slide feet under sandwich, cut sides out.

4. Decorate sandwich with parsley sprigs for feathers.   *Makes 1 sandwich*

Bird-wich

Bagel Dogs with Spicy Red Sauce

    1 cup ketchup
    1 medium onion, finely chopped
    ¼ cup packed brown sugar
    1 tablespoon cider vinegar
    2 teaspoons hot pepper sauce
    1 clove garlic, minced
    1 teaspoon Worcestershire sauce
    1 teaspoon liquid smoke (optional)
    4 bagel dogs

1. Combine all ingredients except bagel dogs in medium saucepan; bring to a boil over medium-high heat. Reduce heat; simmer 5 minutes, stirring occasionally.

2. Prepare bagel dogs according to package directions. Serve with sauce.

Makes 4 servings

Fried Pickle Spears

    3 tablespoons all-purpose flour
    1 teaspoon cornstarch
    3 eggs
    1 cup cornflake crumbs
    12 pickle spears, patted dry
    ½ cup vegetable oil

1. Line serving dish with paper towels; set aside. Combine flour and cornstarch in small bowl. Beat eggs in another small bowl. Place cornflake crumbs in third small bowl.

2. Coat pickle spears in flour mixture, shaking off excess. Dip pickle in eggs; roll in cornflake crumbs. Repeat with remaining pickles.

3. Heat oil in large nonstick skillet over medium heat. Cook four pickles at a time, 1 to 2 minutes per side or until golden brown. Remove to prepared serving dish. Repeat with remaining pickles.

Makes 4 servings

Bagel Dogs with Spicy Red Sauce, Fried Pickle Spears

Indian Corn

¼ cup (½ stick) butter or margarine
1 package (10½ ounces) mini marshmallows
   Yellow food coloring
8 cups peanut butter and chocolate puffed corn cereal
1 cup candy-coated chocolate pieces, divided
10 lollipop sticks*
   Tan and green raffia*

*Lollipop sticks and colored raffia are sold at craft and hobby stores.

1. Line large baking sheet with waxed paper; set aside.

2. Melt butter in large heavy saucepan over low heat. Add marshmallows; stir until melted and smooth. Tint with food coloring until desired shade is reached. Add cereal and ½ cup chocolate pieces; stir until evenly coated. Remove from heat.

3. With lightly greased hands, quickly divide mixture into 10 oblong pieces. Push lollipop stick halfway into each piece; shape like ear of corn. Place on prepared baking sheet. Press remaining ½ cup chocolate pieces into each ear. Let treats stand until set.

4. Tie or tape raffia to lollipop sticks to resemble corn husks.

Makes 10 servings

Indian Corn

Pig-wich

Mayonnaise or mustard
2 round slices deli meat
1½ round cheese slices, divided
1 leaf Boston lettuce
1 round sandwich bun, split
1 black olive
1 slice bologna
1 black bean

1. Layer mayonnaise, deli meat, 1 slice cheese and lettuce on bottom bun. Spread mayonnaise on cut side of top bun and place bun slightly off center on top of lettuce. For feet, slice olive in half lengthwise, then cut small V shape out of bottom of each half. Place olive halves on lettuce, cut side facing out.

2. For snout, cut circle from bologna with round cutter. Cut two small holes in circle just above center. Attach circle to top bun with dab of mayonnaise. For ears, cut two triangles out of bologna. Make two slits in top half of bun 1 inch apart and angling slightly towards sides of bun. Insert triangles into slits.

3. For eyes, cut out two small circles from remaining ½ slice cheese; attach to bun between ears and nose with dabs of mayonnaise. Cut black bean in half; attach cut sides to each cheese circle. For tail, cut long tapered slice of bologna. Attach tail to side of pig and curl.

Makes 1 sandwich

Pig-wich

Quicksand

¾ cup creamy peanut butter
5 ounces cream cheese, softened
1 cup pineapple preserves
⅓ cup milk
1 teaspoon Worcestershire sauce
Dash hot pepper sauce (optional)
1 can (7 ounces) refrigerated breadstick dough (6 breadsticks)
5 rich round crackers, crushed
Cut-up vegetables and fruit for dipping

1. Combine peanut butter and cream cheese in large bowl until well blended. Stir in preserves, milk, Worcestershire and hot pepper sauce, if desired. Transfer to serving bowl or spread in 8- or 9-inch glass pie plate. Cover with plastic wrap; refrigerate until ready to serve.

2. Preheat oven to 375°F. Cut each breadstick in half crosswise; place on ungreased baking sheet. Make 3 slits in one short end of each breadstick half to resemble fingers. Cut small piece of dough from other short end; press dough piece into hand to resemble thumb. Bake 8 to 10 minutes or until golden brown.

3. Just before serving, sprinkle dip with cracker crumbs; serve with breadstick hands, vegetables and fruit. *Makes 12 to 16 servings*

Quicksand

Magic Rainbow Pops

    1 envelope (¼ ounce) unflavored gelatin
¼ cup cold water
½ cup boiling water
    1 carton (6 ounces) raspberry or strawberry yogurt
    1 carton (6 ounces) lemon or orange yogurt
    1 small can (8¼ ounces) apricots or peaches with juice
    Popsicle molds

1. Combine gelatin and cold water in 2-cup glass measuring cup. Let stand 5 minutes to soften. Add boiling water. Stir until gelatin is completely dissolved. Cool slightly.

2. For first layer, combine raspberry yogurt and ¼ cup gelatin mixture in small bowl; stir until completely blended. Fill each popsicle mold about one third full with raspberry mixture.* Freeze 30 to 60 minutes or until slightly frozen.

3. For second layer, combine lemon yogurt with ¼ cup gelatin mixture in small bowl; stir until completely blended. Pour lemon mixture over raspberry layer in each mold.* Freeze 30 to 60 minutes or until slightly frozen.

4. Place apricots with juice and remaining ¼ cup gelatin mixture in blender. Process 20 seconds or until smooth. Pour apricot mixture into each mold.* Cover each pop with mold top; freeze 2 to 5 hours or until pops are firm.

5. To remove pops from molds, place bottom of pop under warm running water for 2 to 3 minutes. Press firmly on bottom to release. (Do not twist or pull the popsicle stick.)

Makes about 6 pops

Pour any extra mixture into small paper cups. Freeze as directed in the tip.

Tip: Three-ounce paper cups can be used in place of the molds. Make the layers as directed or put a single flavor in each cup. Freeze cups about 1 hour, then insert wooden stick (which can be found at craft stores) into the center of each cup. Freeze completely. Peel cup off each pop to serve.

Magic Rainbow Pops

Candy Corn by the Slice

1 package (about 14 ounces) refrigerated pizza crust dough
½ cup (2 ounces) shredded mozzarella cheese
2 cups (8 ounces) shredded Cheddar cheese, divided
⅓ cup pizza sauce

1. Preheat oven to 400°F. Spray 13-inch round pizza pan with nonstick cooking spray. Press dough into pan.

2. Sprinkle mozzarella in 4-inch circle in center of pizza dough. Sprinkle 1 cup Cheddar cheese in 3-inch ring around center circle. Spoon pizza sauce over Cheddar cheese. Create 1½-inch border around edge of pizza with remaining 1 cup Cheddar cheese.

3. Bake 12 to 15 minutes or until edge is lightly browned and cheese is melted and bubbling. Cut into wedges.

Makes 8 slices

Tip

Keeping a couple packages of pizza crust dough on hand is a great way to make sure that a fun snack is only minutes away.

Candy Corn by the Slice

Sweet Surprises

Sweet Sushi

1 package (10½ ounces) marshmallows
3 tablespoons butter
6 cups crisp rice cereal
  Green fruit roll-ups
  Candy fish
  Sliced strawberries, peaches and kiwi

1. Spray 13×9-inch baking pan and spatula with nonstick cooking spray.

2. Place marshmallows and butter in large microwavable bowl; microwave on HIGH 1 to 2 minutes or until melted and smooth, stirring once. Immediately stir in cereal until coated. Press mixture into prepared pan using waxed paper to press into even layer. Let stand 10 minutes.

3. Cut half of cereal bars into 2×1-inch rectangles; round edges of rectangles slightly with hands to form ovals. Cut remaining half of bars into 1½- to 2-inch circles using greased cookie or biscuit cutter.

4. Cut fruit roll-ups into ½-inch-wide and 1-inch-wide strips. Top ovals with candy or fruit; wrap with ½-inch fruit roll-up strips as shown in photo. Wrap 1-inch strips around circles; top with fruit or candy.   *Makes 3 to 4 dozen pieces*

Pretzel Fried Eggs

24 (1-inch) pretzel rings
1 cup white chocolate chips
24 yellow candy-coated chocolate pieces

1. Line baking sheet with waxed paper. Place pretzel rings about 2 inches apart on prepared baking sheet.

2. Place white chocolate chips in medium resealable food storage bag; seal bag. Microwave on HIGH 30 seconds. Knead bag gently and microwave 30 seconds more. Repeat until chips are melted. Cut ¼-inch corner from bag.

3. Squeeze chocolate from bag into center of each pretzel ring in circular motion. Finish with ring of chocolate around edge of pretzel. Use tip of small knife to smooth chocolate, if necessary. Place candy piece in center of each pretzel. Allow to harden at room temperature or refrigerate until set. Store in single layer in airtight container up to 1 week.

Makes 2 dozen eggs

Variation: To make "green eggs and ham," use green candy-coated chocolate pieces for yolks. Cut small pieces of pink fruit leather for ham. Serve 2 Pretzel Fried Eggs with small strips of fruit leather ham and square cinnamon cereal for toast.

Pretzel Fried Eggs

Chocolate Panini Bites

¼ cup chocolate hazelnut spread
4 slices hearty sandwich bread or Italian bread
Nonstick cooking spray

1. Preheat indoor grill.* Spread chocolate hazelnut spread evenly over two slices bread; top with remaining slices.

2. Spray sandwiches lightly with nonstick cooking spray. Grill 2 to 3 minutes or until bread is golden brown. Cut sandwiches into triangles. *Makes 4 servings*

Panini can also be made on the stove in a ridged grill pan or in a nonstick skillet. Cook sandwiches over medium heat about 2 minutes per side.

Chocolate Raspberry Panini Bites: Spread 2 slices bread with raspberry jam or preserves. Spread remaining slices with chocolate hazelnut spread. Cook sandwiches as directed above. *Watch closely because jam burns easily.*

Mini S'mores Pies

6 mini graham cracker pie crusts
½ cup semisweet chocolate chips, divided
¾ cup mini marshmallows

1. Preheat oven to 325°F. Place pie crusts on baking sheet.

2. Divide ¼ cup chocolate chips between pie crusts. Sprinkle marshmallows over chocolate chips. Top with remaining ¼ cup chocolate chips.

3. Bake 3 to 5 minutes or until marshmallows are light golden brown. *Makes 6 servings*

Chocolate Panini Bites

Pound Cake Dip Sticks

½ cup raspberry jam, divided
1 package (10¾ ounces) frozen pound cake
1½ cups cold whipping cream

1. Preheat oven to 400°F. Spray baking sheet with nonstick cooking spray. Microwave ¼ cup jam on HIGH 30 seconds or until smooth.

2. Cut pound cake into 10 (½-inch) slices. Brush one side of slices lightly with warm jam. Cut each slice lengthwise into 3 sticks. Place sticks, jam side up, on prepared baking sheet. Bake 10 minutes or until cake sticks are crisp and light golden brown. Remove to wire rack.

3. Meanwhile, beat whipping cream in large bowl with electric mixer until soft peaks form. Add remaining ¼ cup raspberry jam; beat until combined. Serve pound cake dip sticks with raspberry whipped cream. *Makes 8 to 10 servings*

Chocolate Spiders

1 package (12 ounces) semisweet chocolate chips
1 cup butterscotch chips
¼ cup (½ stick) butter
¼ cup creamy peanut butter
4 cups crisp rice cereal
Chow mein noodles and assorted candies

1. Line baking sheet with waxed paper.

2. Combine chocolate chips, butterscotch chips and butter in large saucepan; stir over medium heat until chips are melted and mixture is well blended. Remove from heat. Add peanut butter; mix well. Add cereal; stir to evenly coat.

3. Drop mixture by tablespoonfuls onto prepared baking sheet; insert chow mein noodles for legs and add candies for eyes. *Makes about 3 dozen*

Doughnut Hole Spiders: Substitute chocolate-covered doughnut holes for shaped cereal mixture. Insert black string licorice, cut into 1½-inch lengths, into doughnut holes for legs. Use desired color decorating icing for eyes.

Pound Cake Dip Sticks

S'more Snack Cake

1 package (about 15 ounces) yellow cake mix, plus ingredients to prepare mix
1 cup chocolate chunks, divided
2½ cups bear-shaped graham crackers, divided
1½ cups mini marshmallows

1. Preheat oven to 350°F. Grease 13×9-inch baking pan.

2. Prepare cake mix according to package directions, adding ½ cup chocolate chunks and 1 cup graham crackers. Spread batter in prepared pan.

3. Bake 30 minutes. Remove cake from oven; sprinkle with remaining ½ cup chocolate chunks and marshmallows. Arrange remaining 1½ cups graham crackers evenly over top.

4. Return cake to oven; bake 8 minutes or until marshmallows are golden brown. Cool completely before cutting.

Makes 24 servings

Tip

This cake is best served the day it is made. Keep leftovers in an airtight container.

S'more Snack Cake

Magic Minis

Banana Split Ice Cream Sandwiches

1 package (about 16 ounces) refrigerated chocolate chip cookie dough
2 bananas, mashed
½ cup strawberry jam, divided
4 cups strawberry ice cream, softened
   Hot fudge topping
   Whipped cream
9 maraschino cherries

1. Let dough stand at room temperature 15 minutes. Preheat oven to 350°F. Lightly grease 13×9-inch baking pan.

2. Beat dough and bananas in large bowl with electric mixer at medium speed until well blended. Spread dough evenly in prepared pan; smooth top. Bake 22 minutes or until edges are lightly browned. Cool completely in pan on wire rack.

3. Line 8-inch square baking pan with foil or plastic wrap, allowing some to hang over edges of pan. Remove cooled cookie from pan; cut in half crosswise. Place 1 cookie half, top side down, in 8-inch pan, trimming edges to fit, if necessary. Spread ¼ cup jam evenly over cookie. Spread ice cream evenly over jam. Spread remaining ¼ cup jam over bottom of remaining cookie half; place jam side down over ice cream. Wrap tightly with foil; freeze at least 2 hours or overnight.

4. Cut into bars and top with hot fudge topping, whipped cream and cherries.

Makes 9 servings

Petite Pudding Parfaits

2 ounces bittersweet or semisweet chocolate, chopped (or about ⅓ cup chips)
2 ounces white chocolate, chopped (or about ⅓ cup chips)
½ cup sugar
2 tablespoons flour
1 tablespoon cornstarch
⅛ teaspoon salt
2¼ cups milk
2 egg yolks, beaten
2 teaspoons vanilla
Chocolate curls or grated bittersweet chocolate (optional)

1. Place bittersweet chocolate and white chocolate in separate heatproof bowls; set aside.

2. Combine sugar, flour, cornstarch and salt in small saucepan. Gradually whisk in milk. Cook over medium heat until mixture comes to a boil, stirring constantly. Boil 2 minutes, stirring constantly.

3. Remove saucepan from heat. Stir small amount of hot mixture into egg yolks; return egg yolk mixture to saucepan. Cook and stir over low heat until thickened. Remove from heat; stir in vanilla.

4. Spoon half of egg yolk mixture over each chocolate; stir until melted.

5. For 2-ounce shot glasses, alternate layers of puddings using about 1 tablespoon pudding for each layer. Cover and refrigerate until chilled. Top with chocolate curls before serving, if desired.

Makes about 8 servings

Petite Pudding Parfaits

Mini Strawberry Shortcakes

1 quart strawberries, hulled and sliced
½ cup sugar, divided
1 cup all-purpose flour
2 teaspoons baking powder
¼ teaspoon salt
¼ cup (½ stick) butter, cubed
1¼ cups whipping cream, divided

1. Combine strawberries and ¼ cup sugar in medium bowl; set aside.

2. Preheat oven to 425°F. Whisk flour, 2 tablespoons sugar, baking powder and salt in large bowl. Cut in butter with pastry blender or two knives until mixture resembles coarse crumbs. Gradually add ½ cup cream, stirring gently until dough comes together. (Dough will be slightly sticky.) Knead gently 4 to 6 times.

3. Pat dough into 6-inch square on lightly floured surface. Cut dough into 1½-inch squares with sharp knife. Place 1½ inches apart on ungreased baking sheet.

4. Bake 10 minutes or until golden brown. Remove to wire rack; cool slightly.

5. Meanwhile, beat remaining ¾ cup cream and 2 tablespoons sugar in small bowl with electric mixer at high speed until soft peaks form.

6. Split biscuits in half horizontally. Top bottom halves of biscuits with berry mixture, whipped cream and top halves of biscuits.

Makes 16 mini shortcakes

Mini Strawberry Shortcakes

Little Chocolate Chip Coffee Cakes

1⅓ cups all-purpose flour
¾ teaspoon baking powder
½ teaspoon salt
¼ teaspoon baking soda
¾ cup packed brown sugar
½ cup (1 stick) butter, softened
¼ cup granulated sugar
1 teaspoon vanilla
2 eggs
½ cup plus 3 tablespoons milk, divided
1½ cups semisweet chocolate chips, divided

1. Preheat oven to 350°F. Generously grease and flour 18 mini (¼-cup) bundt cups. Whisk flour, baking powder, salt and baking soda in small bowl.

2. Beat brown sugar, butter, granulated sugar and vanilla in large bowl with electric mixer at medium speed until light and fluffy. Beat in eggs, one at a time, until well blended. Alternately add flour mixture and ½ cup milk, beginning and ending with flour mixture, beating until blended after each addition. Stir in 1 cup chocolate chips. Spoon batter into prepared bundt cups, filling three-fourths full (about 3 tablespoons batter per cup).

3. Bake 16 minutes or until toothpick inserted into centers comes out clean. Cool in pan 5 minutes; invert onto wire racks to cool completely.

4. Combine remaining ½ cup chocolate chips and 3 tablespoons milk in small microwavable bowl. Microwave on HIGH 30 seconds; stir. Microwave at 15-second intervals until melted and smooth. Drizzle over cakes. *Makes 18 coffee cakes*

Little Chocolate Chip Coffee Cakes

Jelly Doughnut Bites

½ cup plus 3 tablespoons warm (95 to 105°F) milk, divided
1¼ teaspoons active dry yeast
⅓ cup granulated sugar
1 tablespoon butter, softened
2½ cups all-purpose flour
1 egg
½ teaspoon salt
½ cup raspberry jam
Powdered sugar

1. Combine 3 tablespoons warm milk and yeast in large bowl. Let stand 5 minutes. Add granulated sugar, butter and remaining ½ cup milk; mix well. Add flour, egg and salt; beat with dough hook of electric mixer at medium speed until dough starts to climb up dough hook. If dough is too sticky, add additional flour, 1 tablespoon at a time.

2. Transfer dough to greased medium bowl; turn dough over to grease top. Cover and let stand in warm place 1 hour.

3. Grease 48 mini (1¾-inch) muffin cups. Punch down dough. Shape pieces of dough into 1-inch balls; place in prepared muffin cups. Cover and let stand 1 hour. Preheat oven to 375°F.

4. Bake 10 minutes or until golden brown. Remove to wire racks; cool completely.

5. Place jam in pastry bag fitted with small round tip. Insert tip into side of each doughnut; squeeze about 1 teaspoon jam into center. Sprinkle filled doughnuts with powdered sugar.

Makes 48 doughnut bites

Tip: These doughnuts are best eaten the same day they are made. They can be served warm or at room temperature. If desired, microwave on HIGH 10 seconds just before serving.

Jelly Doughnut Bites

Carrot Cake Minis

1 cup packed light brown sugar
¾ cup plus 2 tablespoons all-purpose flour
1 teaspoon baking soda
½ teaspoon salt
½ teaspoon ground cinnamon
¼ teaspoon ground nutmeg
⅛ teaspoon ground cloves
½ cup canola oil
2 eggs
1½ cups lightly packed grated carrots
½ teaspoon vanilla
Cream Cheese Frosting (recipe follows)
Toasted shredded coconut (optional)

1. Preheat oven to 350°F. Line 36 mini (1¾-inch) muffin cups with paper baking cups.

2. Whisk brown sugar, flour, baking soda, salt, cinnamon, nutmeg and cloves in large bowl. Stir in oil until blended. Add eggs, one at a time, stirring until blended after each addition. Stir in carrots and vanilla. Spoon batter evenly into prepared muffin cups.

3. Bake 15 minutes or until toothpick inserted into centers comes out clean. Cool in pans 5 minutes. Remove to wire racks; cool completely.

4. Meanwhile, prepare Cream Cheese Frosting. Frost cupcakes. Sprinkle with coconut, if desired. Cover and store in refrigerator.

Makes 36 mini cupcakes

Cream Cheese Frosting: Beat 1 package (8 ounces) softened cream cheese and ¼ cup (½ stick) softened butter in medium bowl with electric mixer at medium-high speed until creamy. Gradually beat in 1½ cups sifted powdered sugar until well blended. Beat in ¼ teaspoon salt and ¼ teaspoon vanilla. Makes about 3 cups.

Tip: Use a food processor to quickly grate the carrots for this recipe. Use the metal blade and pulse the carrots until they are evenly grated.

Carrot Cake Minis

Brownie Ice Cream Treats

½ cup all-purpose flour
½ teaspoon salt
¼ teaspoon baking powder
6 tablespoons butter
1 cup sugar
½ cup unsweetened Dutch process cocoa powder
2 eggs
½ teaspoon vanilla
2 cups pistachio or favorite flavor ice cream, slightly softened
Hot fudge topping, heated (optional)

1. Preheat oven to 350°F. Spray 9-inch square baking pan with nonstick cooking spray. Whisk flour, salt and baking powder in small bowl.

2. Melt butter in medium saucepan over low heat. Stir in sugar until blended. Stir in cocoa until well blended. Stir in eggs, one at a time, then vanilla. Stir in flour mixture until blended. Pour into prepared pan.

3. Bake 20 minutes or until toothpick inserted into center comes out with fudgy crumbs. Cool completely in pan on wire rack.

4. For 2¼-inch-wide jars, cut out 16 brownies using 2-inch round cookie or biscuit cutter. (See Tip.) Remove brownie scraps from pan (any pieces left between round cut-outs); crumble into small pieces. (Save remaining brownies for another use.)

5. Place 1 brownie in each of eight ½-cup glass jars. Top with 2 tablespoons ice cream, pressing to form flat layer over brownie. Repeat brownie and ice cream layers.

6. Drizzle with hot fudge topping, if desired. Sprinkle with brownie crumbs. Serve immediately. (Or make ahead, omitting hot fudge topping. Cover and freeze until ready to serve.)   *Makes 8 servings*

Tip: Measure the diameter of your jar first and cut out your brownies slightly smaller to fit in the jar. If your jars are too short to fit 2 brownie layers, cut the brownies in half horizontally with a serrated knife.

Brownie Ice Cream Treats

Chocolate Chip S'more Bites

    1 package (about 16 ounces) refrigerated chocolate chip cookie dough
  ¾ cup semisweet chocolate chips
  ¼ cup plus 2 tablespoons whipping cream
  ½ cup marshmallow creme
  ½ cup sour cream

1. Preheat oven to 325°F. Spray 13×9-inch baking pan with nonstick cooking spray.

2. Press cookie dough into prepared pan, using damp hands to spread dough into even layer and cover bottom of pan. (Layer of dough will be very thin.) Bake 20 minutes or until light golden brown and just set. Cool completely in pan on wire rack.

3. Meanwhile, place chocolate chips in medium heatproof bowl. Place cream in small microwavable bowl; microwave on HIGH 1 minute or just until simmering. Pour cream over chocolate chips. Let stand 2 minutes; stir until smooth. Let stand 10 minutes or until thickened.

4. Combine marshmallow creme and sour cream in small bowl until smooth.

5. Cut bars into 1¼-inch squares with sharp knife. For each s'more, spread scant teaspoon chocolate mixture on bottom of one square; spread scant teaspoon marshmallow mixture on bottom of second square. Press together to form s'mores.   *Makes about 4 dozen s'mores*

Chocolate Chip S'more Bites

Adorable Animals

Cookie Dough Bears

1 package (about 16 ounces) refrigerated sugar cookie dough
1 cup uncooked quick oats
   Mini semisweet chocolate chips

1. Let dough stand at room temperature 15 minutes. Combine dough and oats in medium bowl; beat with electric mixer at medium speed until blended. Cover and freeze 15 minutes.

2. Preheat oven to 350°F. Lightly coat cookie sheets with nonstick cooking spray. For each bear, shape 1 (1-inch) ball for body and 1 (¾-inch) ball for head. Place body and head together on cookie sheets; flatten slightly. Form 7 small balls for arms, legs, ears and nose; arrange on bear body and head. Place 2 chocolate chips on each head for eyes. Place 1 chocolate chip on each body for belly button.

3. Bake 12 to 14 minutes or until edges are lightly browned. Cool on cookie sheets 2 minutes. Remove to wire racks; cool completely.

Makes about 9 cookies

Tip

To make these delicious bears even more fun, try embellishing them with assorted decorating gels. Add a bow tie or a hair bow. Get creative!

Mischievous Monkeys

    3 cups all-purpose flour
    $\frac{1}{2}$ cup unsweetened cocoa powder
    1 teaspoon salt
    $1\frac{1}{2}$ cups sugar
    1 cup (2 sticks) unsalted butter, softened
    2 eggs
    1 teaspoon vanilla
      Yellow gel food coloring
    1 cup prepared white or vanilla frosting
      Black string licorice
   20 brown candy-coated peanut butter candies

1. Whisk flour, cocoa and salt in medium bowl. Beat sugar and butter in large bowl with electric mixer at medium speed until light and fluffy. Add eggs, 1 at a time, beating until blended after each addition. Add vanilla; beat until blended. Gradually add flour mixture, beating until blended after each addition. Divide dough evenly into 2 discs. Wrap and refrigerate 1 hour.

2. Preheat oven to 350°F. Line cookie sheets with parchment paper. Working with 1 disc at a time, roll out dough between parchment paper to $\frac{3}{8}$-inch thickness. From each disc, cut out 5 large circles with 3-inch round cookie cutter, 5 medium circles with 2-inch round cookie cutter and 10 small circles with $1\frac{1}{2}$-inch round cookie cutter.

3. Place large circles 3 inches apart on prepared cookie sheets. Place 2 small circles next to each large circle for ears. Place medium circles 1 inch apart on separate prepared cookie sheet. Refrigerate 15 minutes.

4. Bake large circles 15 to 17 minutes or until set. Bake medium circles 12 to 15 minutes or until set. Cool on cookie sheets 5 minutes. Remove to wire racks; cool completely.

5. Add food coloring, a few drops at a time, to frosting; stir until evenly colored. Spread medium circles with frosting. Cut lengths of licorice for nose and mouth; press into frosting. Let stand 10 minutes or until set. Spread thin layer of frosting on back of medium circles and adhere to large circles for mouth. Spread small circle of frosting on inside of each small circle for ears. Dot back of 2 candies with frosting; adhere to each large circle just above medium circle for eyes. Let stand 10 minutes or until set.

Makes 10 cookies

Mischievous Monkeys

Tasty Turtles

3½ cups all-purpose flour
½ teaspoon salt
1½ cups sugar
1 cup (2 sticks) unsalted butter, softened
2 eggs
2 teaspoons vanilla
Green gel food coloring
144 green gumdrops
Green, black and red decorating gels
Brown candy-coated chocolate pieces
Brown mini candy-coated chocolate pieces

1. Whisk flour and salt in medium bowl. Beat sugar and butter in large bowl with electric mixer at medium speed until light and fluffy. Add eggs, 1 at a time, beating until blended after each addition. Add vanilla; beat until blended.

2. Gradually add flour mixture, beating until blended after each addition. Add food coloring, a few drops at a time, to dough; beat until evenly colored. Divide dough evenly into 2 discs. Wrap and refrigerate 1 hour.

3. Preheat oven to 350°F. Line cookie sheets with parchment paper. Working with 1 disc at a time, cut each disc into 36 even pieces. Roll each piece into a ball; flatten slightly. Place 1 inch apart on prepared cookie sheets. Refrigerate 15 minutes. Bake 12 to 15 minutes or until set. Cool on cookie sheets 5 minutes. Remove to wire racks; cool completely.

4. Reserve 72 gumdrops. Cut remaining gumdrops into quarters. Dot back of gumdrop pieces with green decorating gel and adhere to sides of cookies for legs. Dot bottom of reserved gumdrops with green decorating gel and adhere 1 to each cookie for head. Dot back of 3 chocolate pieces with green decorating gel and adhere to center of each cookie. Dot back of mini chocolate pieces with green decorating gel and adhere to create remainder of shell.

5. Pipe eyes, nose and mouth on each head using black and red decorating gels. Let stand 10 minutes or until set.

Makes 6 dozen cookies

Tasty Turtles

Zebras

2 packages (about 16 ounces each) refrigerated sugar cookie dough
½ cup all-purpose flour
½ cup unsweetened Dutch process cocoa powder
Prepared dark chocolate frosting
Assorted sprinkles
Mini semisweet chocolate chips and semisweet chocolate chips

1. Let doughs stand at room temperature 15 minutes.

2. Combine 1 package dough and flour in large bowl; beat with electric mixer at medium speed until well blended. Combine remaining package dough and cocoa in another large bowl; beat at medium speed until well blended. Form each dough into disc; wrap and freeze 15 minutes.

3. Working with 1 disc at a time, roll out dough between parchment paper into 9-inch square. Place cocoa dough on top of plain dough. Cut into 4 (4½-inch) squares. Layer squares on top of each other, alternating cocoa and plain doughs. Wrap and refrigerate at least 4 hours or up to 2 days.

4. Preheat oven to 350°F. Lightly grease cookie sheets. Trim edges of dough to make square. Cut dough into ¼-inch striped slices, wiping off knife after each cut; cut slices in half to make 2¼×2-inch rectangles. Place rectangles 2 inches apart on prepared cookie sheets.

5. Working with stripes vertically, cut small triangle from top left corner and narrow triangle from top right edge of each rectangle. Discard scraps. Cut small triangle from center of bottom edge; place at top of cookie for ear.

6. Bake 10 minutes or until edges are light brown. Cool on cookie sheets 5 minutes. Remove to wire racks; cool completely.

7. For manes, spread frosting on cookie edges at both sides of ear; top with sprinkles. Attach 1 mini chocolate chip for eye and 1 chocolate chip for nostril to each cookie with frosting.

Makes about 3 dozen cookies

Zebras

Snickerpoodles

1 package (about 16 ounces) refrigerated sugar cookie dough
1 teaspoon ground cinnamon, divided
1 teaspoon vanilla
¼ cup sugar
Semisweet chocolate chips and mini semisweet chocolate chips
White and pink decorating icings

1. Let dough stand at room temperature 15 minutes. Lightly grease cookie sheets.

2. Preheat oven to 350°F. Combine dough, ½ teaspoon cinnamon and vanilla in large bowl; beat with electric mixer at medium speed until well blended. Combine sugar and remaining ½ teaspoon cinnamon in small bowl. For each poodle face, shape 1½ teaspoons dough into oval. Roll in cinnamon-sugar mixture; place on prepared cookie sheets.

3. For poodle ears, divide 1½ teaspoons dough in half; shape each half into teardrop shape. Roll in cinnamon-sugar mixture; place at either side of face.

4. For top of poodle head, shape scant teaspoon dough into oval. Roll in cinnamon-sugar mixture; place at top of face.

5. Bake 10 to 12 minutes or until edges are lightly browned. Immediately press 1 chocolate chip upside down onto each face for nose. Cool on cookie sheets 2 minutes. Remove to wire racks; cool completely.

6. Pipe 2 small circles on each face with white decorating icing. Press mini chocolate chips into icing for eyes. Decorate as desired with white and pink icings.

Makes about 2 dozen cookies

Snickerpoodles

Luscious Lions

Manes

    1 package (about 16 ounces) refrigerated sugar cookie dough
$\frac{1}{4}$ cup all-purpose flour
  2 tablespoons powdered sugar
    Grated peel of 1 large orange
$\frac{1}{4}$ teaspoon yellow gel food coloring
$\frac{1}{4}$ teaspoon red gel food coloring

Faces

    1 package (about 16 ounces) refrigerated sugar cookie dough
$\frac{1}{4}$ cup all-purpose flour
  2 tablespoons powdered sugar
    Grated peel of 2 lemons
$\frac{1}{2}$ teaspoon yellow gel food coloring
    Mini candy-coated chocolate pieces
    White decorating icing
    Assorted decors
    Brown decorating icing or melted chocolate

1. For manes, let 1 package dough stand at room temperature 15 minutes. Generously grease 2 cookie sheets.

2. Combine dough, $\frac{1}{4}$ cup flour, 2 tablespoons powdered sugar, orange peel, $\frac{1}{4}$ teaspoon yellow food coloring and red food coloring in large bowl; beat with electric mixer at medium speed until well blended. Shape into 24 balls. Place on prepared cookie sheets; flatten into $2\frac{3}{4}$-inch circles. Cut each circle with $2\frac{1}{2}$-inch fluted round cookie cutter. Discard scraps. Refrigerate 30 minutes.

3. Preheat oven to 350°F. Bake 12 to 14 minutes or until lightly browned. Cool on cookie sheets 2 minutes. Remove to wire racks; cool completely.

4. For faces, let 1 package dough stand at room temperature 15 minutes. Generously grease 2 cookie sheets.

5. Combine dough, ¼ cup flour, 2 tablespoons powdered sugar, lemon peel and ½ teaspoon yellow food coloring in another large bowl; beat with electric mixer at medium speed until well blended. Shape into 24 balls. Place on prepared cookie sheets; flatten into 1¾-inch circles. Cut each circle with 1½-inch round cookie cutter. Remove dough scraps; shape into ears. Attach 2 ears to each face. Place 1 chocolate piece in center of each ear and 1 chocolate piece on face for nose.

6. Bake 14 minutes or until lightly browned. Cool on cookie sheets 2 minutes. Remove to wire racks; cool completely.

7. Attach faces to manes with white decorating icing. Pipe 2 small circles on each face with white icing. Press decors into icing for eyes. Pipe whiskers using brown icing.

Makes 2 dozen cookies

Peppermint Pigs

    1 package (about 16 ounces) refrigerated sugar cookie dough
    ½ cup all-purpose flour
    ¾ teaspoon peppermint extract
       Red food coloring
       White decorating icing and mini candy-coated chocolate pieces

1. Let dough stand at room temperature 15 minutes. Lightly grease cookie sheets.

2. Preheat oven to 350°F. Combine dough, flour, peppermint extract and food coloring in large bowl; beat with electric mixer at medium speed until well blended. Divide dough into 20 equal pieces.

3. Shape each dough piece into 1 (1-inch) ball, 1 (½-inch) ball and 2 (¼-inch) balls. Flatten 1-inch ball into ¼-inch-thick circle; place on prepared cookie sheets. Flatten ½-inch ball into ¼-inch-thick oval; place on top of circle for snout. Shape 2 (¼-inch) balls into triangles; fold point over and place at top of circle for ears. Make indentations in snout for nostrils with toothpick.

4. Bake 9 to 11 minutes or until set. Cool on cookie sheets 2 minutes. Remove to wire racks; cool completely. Pipe 2 small circles on each face with white decorating icing. Press chocolate pieces into icing for eyes.

Makes 20 cookies

Citrus Easter Chicks

    1 package (about 16 ounces) refrigerated sugar cookie dough
    1/3 cup all-purpose flour
    1 1/2 to 2 teaspoons lemon extract
       Lemon Cookie Glaze (recipe follows)
    2 cups shredded coconut, tinted yellow*
       Mini semisweet chocolate chips, assorted candies and decors

*To tint coconut, combine small amount of food coloring (paste, gel or liquid) with 1 teaspoon water in large bowl. Add coconut and stir until evenly coated. Add more food coloring, if needed.

1. Let dough stand at room temperature 15 minutes. Combine dough, flour and lemon extract in large bowl; beat with electric mixer at medium speed until well blended. Divide dough evenly into 2 discs. Wrap and refrigerate 1 hour.

2. Preheat oven to 350°F. Working with 1 disc at a time, roll out dough between parchment paper to 1/4-inch thickness. Cut out shapes with 2- to 3-inch chick cookie cutters. Place 2 inches apart on ungreased cookie sheets.

3. Bake 7 to 9 minutes or until set. Cool on cookie sheets 5 minutes. Remove to wire racks; cool completely.

4. Place wire racks over parchment paper. Prepare Lemon Cookie Glaze; spread over tops of cookies. Sprinkle with coconut. Decorate chicks with chocolate chips, candies and decors as desired. Let stand 40 minutes or until set.   *Makes about 1 1/2 dozen cookies*

Lemon Cookie Glaze

    4 cups powdered sugar
    1/2 teaspoon grated lemon peel
    4 to 6 tablespoons lemon juice
       Yellow food coloring

Combine powdered sugar, lemon peel and lemon juice, 1 tablespoon at a time, in medium bowl to make pourable glaze. Add food coloring, a few drops at a time; stir until evenly colored.   *Makes about 2 cups*

Citrus Easter Chicks

Kitty Cookies

1 package (about 16 ounces) refrigerated sugar cookie dough
   White Decorating Frosting (recipe follows)
   Assorted food colorings
   Assorted colored candies and red licorice

1. Preheat oven to 350°F. Reserve half of dough; wrap and refrigerate.

2. Roll out remaining dough between parchment paper to ⅛-inch thickness. Cut out shapes using 3½-inch kitty face cookie cutter. Place 2 inches apart on ungreased cookie sheets. Repeat with reserved dough and scraps.

3. Bake 8 to 10 minutes or until set. Cool on cookie sheets 2 minutes. Remove to wire racks; cool completely.

4. Prepare White Decorating Frosting. Tint with food colorings as desired. Decorate with frosting and assorted candies as desired. Cut licorice into short pieces and press into frosting for whiskers.   *Makes about 1½ dozen cookies*

White Decorating Frosting

4 cups powdered sugar
½ cup shortening or unsalted butter
1 tablespoon corn syrup
6 to 8 tablespoons milk

Beat powdered sugar, shortening, corn syrup and milk in medium bowl with electric mixer at high speed 2 minutes or until fluffy.   *Makes about 2 cups*

Kitty Cookies

Octo-Cookies

    1 package (about 16 ounces) refrigerated chocolate chip cookie dough
    ¼ cup all-purpose flour
    10 whole almonds
        Powdered Sugar Glaze (recipe follows)
        Assorted food colorings
        White decorating icing and assorted candies

1. Let dough stand at room temperature 15 minutes. Grease 10 mini (1¾-inch) muffin cups. Combine dough and flour in large bowl; beat with electric mixer at medium speed until well blended. Reserve two thirds of dough; wrap and refrigerate.

2. Preheat oven to 350°F. For heads, divide remaining one third of dough into 10 equal pieces. Place almond in center of each piece; shape into balls, covering nuts completely. Place in prepared muffin cups; freeze 10 minutes. Bake 10 minutes or until set. Gently loosen cookies around edges; cool in pan 10 minutes. Remove to wire rack; cool completely.

3. For legs, divide reserved dough into 10 equal pieces. Divide each piece equally into 8 pieces; shape each piece into 1½- to 2-inch-long rope. Shape tips at one end to a point. Arrange groups of 8 legs on ungreased cookie sheets with thicker end of legs touching in center and pointed ends about ¼ inch away from each other at outside of circular shape. Bake 6 to 8 minutes or until set. Cool completely on cookie sheets.

4. Place wire racks over waxed paper. Carefully transfer legs to wire racks. Prepare Powdered Sugar Glaze; tint glaze with food colorings as desired. Attach heads to legs using glaze; let stand 15 minutes or until set. Spread remaining glaze over cookies. Let stand 40 minutes or until set. Decorate with white decorating icing and candies as desired.   *Makes 10 cookies*

Powdered Sugar Glaze

    2 cups powdered sugar
    6 to 9 tablespoons whipping cream, divided

Whisk powdered sugar and 6 tablespoons cream in medium bowl until smooth. Add remaining cream, 1 tablespoon at a time, to make pourable glaze.   *Makes about 1 cup*

Octo-Cookies

Panda Pals

3½ cups all-purpose flour
1 teaspoon salt
1½ cups sugar
1 cup (2 sticks) unsalted butter, softened
2 eggs
1 teaspoon almond extract
1 teaspoon vanilla
1 cup prepared white or vanilla frosting
Black gel food coloring
Black jelly beans, cut in half

1. Whisk flour and salt in medium bowl. Beat sugar and butter in large bowl with electric mixer at medium speed until light and fluffy. Add eggs, 1 at a time, beating until blended after each addition. Add almond extract and vanilla; beat until blended.

2. Gradually add flour mixture, beating until blended after each addition. Divide dough evenly into 2 discs. Wrap and refrigerate 1 hour.

3. Preheat oven to 350°F. Line cookie sheets with parchment paper. Working with 1 disc at a time, roll out dough between parchment paper to ³⁄₈-inch thickness. From each disc, cut out 6 large circles with 3-inch round cookie cutter, 6 medium circles with 1¾-inch round cookie cutter and 12 small circles with 1¼-inch round cookie cutter.

4. Place large circles 3 inches apart on prepared cookie sheets. Place 2 small circles next to each large circle for ears. Place medium circles 1 inch apart on separate prepared cookie sheet. Refrigerate 15 minutes.

5. Bake large circles 15 to 17 minutes or until set. Bake medium circles 12 to 15 minutes or until set. Cool on cookie sheets 5 minutes. Remove to wire racks; cool completely.

6. Spread medium circles with frosting; spread thin layer of frosting on backs and adhere to large circles for mouth. Add food coloring, a few drops at a time, to remaining frosting; stir until evenly colored. Spread small circles with black frosting for ears. Dot cut side of jelly beans with frosting and adhere for eyes and nose. Pipe mouth using black frosting. Let stand 10 minutes or until set.

Makes 1 dozen cookies

Panda Pals

Just For Kids

Building Blocks

1 package (about 16 ounces) refrigerated cookie dough, any flavor
Powdered Sugar Glaze (recipe follows)
Assorted food colorings
Assorted small round gummy candies (about ¼ inch in diameter)

1. Let dough stand at room temperature 15 minutes. Grease 13×9-inch baking pan.

2. Preheat oven to 350°F. Press dough evenly into bottom of prepared pan. Score dough lengthwise and crosswise into 32 equal rectangles (about 2¼×1½ inches each). Freeze 10 minutes.

3. Bake 10 minutes. Re-score partially baked cookies. Bake 4 to 5 minutes or until edges are lightly browned and center is set. Cut through score marks to separate cookies. Cool in pan 10 minutes. Remove to wire rack; cool completely.

4. Prepare Powdered Sugar Glaze; tint glaze with food colorings as desired. Place wire racks over waxed paper. Spread glaze over tops and sides of cookies. Let stand 5 minutes. Attach 6 gummy candies to each cookie. Let stand 40 minutes or until set. *Makes 32 cookies*

Powdered Sugar Glaze

2 cups powdered sugar
6 to 9 tablespoons whipping cream, divided

Whisk powdered sugar and 6 tablespoons cream in medium bowl until smooth. Add remaining cream, 1 tablespoon at a time, to make pourable glaze. *Makes about 1 cup*

Cookie Caterpillars

Easy All-Purpose Cookie Dough (recipe follows)
1 cup chocolate hazelnut spread
White chocolate chips, decors, red licorice strings and candy-coated chocolate pieces

1. Prepare Easy All-Purpose Cookie Dough.

2. Preheat oven to 300°F. Roll out dough between parchment paper to ¼-inch thickness. Cut out circles with 1¼-inch round cookie cutter. Place 1 inch apart on ungreased cookie sheets.

3. Bake 12 to 15 minutes or until tops of cookies are dry to the touch. Cool on cookie sheets 1 minute. Remove to wire racks; cool completely.

4. Assemble caterpillars by attaching 7 or 8 cookies together, using chocolate hazelnut spread as "glue" between cookies. Create faces, antennae and legs on caterpillars with chocolate chips, decors, licorice strings and chocolate pieces.   *Makes 12 caterpillars*

Easy All-Purpose Cookie Dough

1 cup (2 sticks) butter, softened
½ cup powdered sugar
2 tablespoons packed light brown sugar
¼ teaspoon salt
¼ cup unsweetened Dutch process cocoa powder
1 egg
2 cups all-purpose flour

1. Beat butter, powdered sugar, brown sugar and salt in large bowl with electric mixer at medium speed 2 minutes or until light and fluffy. Add cocoa and egg; beat until well blended.

2. Add flour, ½ cup at a time, beating well after each addition. Shape dough into disc; wrap and refrigerate 1 hour.

Cookie Caterpillars

Peanut Butter Aliens

    1 package (about 16 ounces) refrigerated sugar cookie dough
    ½ cup creamy peanut butter
    ⅓ cup all-purpose flour
    ¼ cup powdered sugar
    ½ teaspoon vanilla
       Green decorating icing
    1 cup strawberry jam

1. Let dough stand at room temperature 15 minutes. Grease 2 cookie sheets.

2. Preheat oven to 350°F. Combine dough, peanut butter, flour, powdered sugar and vanilla in large bowl; beat with electric mixer at medium speed until well blended. Reserve half of dough; wrap and refrigerate.

3. Roll out remaining dough between parchment paper to ¼-inch thickness. Cut out 14 circles with 3-inch round cookie cutter; pinch 1 side of each circle to make teardrop shape. Place 2 inches apart on prepared cookie sheets. Bake 12 to 14 minutes or until set. Cool on cookie sheets 2 minutes. Remove to wire racks; cool completely.

4. Roll out reserved dough between parchment paper to ¼-inch thickness. Cut out 14 circles with 3-inch round cookie cutter; pinch 1 side of each circle to form teardrop shape. Place 2 inches apart on prepared cookie sheets. Cut out 2 oblong holes for eyes. Make small slit for mouth. Bake 12 to 14 minutes or until set. Cool on cookie sheets 2 minutes. Remove to wire racks; cool completely.

5. Spread icing on cookies with faces; let stand 10 minutes or until set. Spread jam on uncut cookies. Top each jam-topped cookie with green face cookie.   *Makes 14 sandwich cookies*

Peanut Butter Aliens

Magic Number Cookies

3½ cups all-purpose flour
1 teaspoon salt
1½ cups sugar
1 cup (2 sticks) unsalted butter, softened
2 eggs
2 teaspoons vanilla
Fuchsia and teal gel food colorings

1. Whisk flour and salt in medium bowl.

2. Beat sugar and butter in large bowl with electric mixer at medium speed until light and fluffy. Add eggs, 1 at a time, beating until blended after each addition. Add vanilla; beat until blended.

3. Gradually add flour mixture, beating until blended after each addition. Divide dough in half; place in separate medium bowls. Add fuchsia food coloring, a few drops at a time, to half of dough; beat until evenly colored. Add teal food coloring, a few drops at a time, to remaining half of dough; beat until evenly colored. Shape each dough into disc; wrap and refrigerate 1 hour.

4. Preheat oven to 350°F. Line cookie sheets with parchment paper. Working with 1 disc at a time, roll out dough between parchment paper to ⅜-inch thickness. Cut out stars with 4½-inch cookie cutter. Place 1 inch apart on prepared cookie sheets. Cut out number from center of each star using 2-inch cookie cutter. Transfer fuchsia numbers to teal stars and teal numbers to fuchsia stars. Refrigerate 15 minutes.

5. Bake 15 to 17 minutes or until set. Cool on cookie sheets 5 minutes. Remove to wire racks; cool completely.

Makes about 14 cookies

Magic Number Cookies

Magic Lightning Bolts

1 package (about 16 ounces) refrigerated sugar cookie dough
  Blue food coloring
1 cup prepared cream cheese frosting
  Blue crackling candy or blue decorating sugar

1. Grease cookie sheets. Reserve half of dough; wrap and refrigerate.

2. Roll out remaining half of dough between parchment paper to ¼-inch thickness. Cut into zigzag lightning shapes about ½ inch wide and 5½ inches long. Place 2 inches apart on prepared cookie sheets. Repeat with reserved dough and scraps. Refrigerate 1 hour.

3. Preheat oven to 350°F. Bake 5 to 7 minutes or until edges are lightly browned. Cool on cookie sheets 2 minutes. Remove to wire racks; cool completely.

4. Just before serving, add food coloring, a few drops at a time, to frosting; stir until well blended. Spread frosting on cookies. Sprinkle crackling candy over frosting.

Makes about 2 dozen cookies

Tip
If using crackling candy, do not frost and decorate cookies in advance. Crackling candy begins to lose its popping quality when it is exposed to air and moisture.

Magic Lightning Bolts

Chocolate Railroad Cookies

  2 cups all-purpose flour
¾ cup sugar
½ cup unsweetened cocoa powder
⅛ teaspoon salt
  1 cup (2 sticks) unsalted butter, slightly softened, cut into ½-inch pieces

1. Beat flour, sugar, cocoa and salt in large bowl with electric mixer at low speed until well combined. With mixer running, add butter, 1 piece at a time, beating until mixture looks moist and crumbly.

2. Knead dough with hands until butter is well incorporated. Divide dough in half. Shape each half into rough square; wrap and refrigerate 30 minutes.

3. Line 2 cookie sheets with parchment paper. Working with 1 square at a time, roll out dough between parchment paper into 10×6-inch rectangle (about ¼ inch thick). Trim edges, reserving scraps.

4. To make rails, cut 2 (¼-inch-wide) strips from the 10-inch side of the rectangle. Place parallel to each other, ½ inch apart, on prepared cookie sheet.

5. To make ties, cut off 2 more ¼-inch-wide strips of dough. Cut each strip into 6 pieces (each about 1½ inches long). Press 9 evenly spaced ties across rails. Reserve remaining 3 ties.

6. Repeat with remaining dough and reserved scraps to create 6 more railroad tracks. Refrigerate 15 minutes.

7. Preheat oven to 350°F. Cut each whole track into 3 separate tracks (3 ties per track), creating 42 cookies total. Arrange cookies ½ inch apart on prepared cookie sheets.

8. Bake 12 to 15 minutes or until set. Cool completely on cookie sheets.   *Makes 42 cookies*

Chocolate Railroad Cookies

Sour Spirals

1 package (about 16 ounces) refrigerated sugar cookie dough
2 tablespoons plus 1½ teaspoons blue raspberry-flavored gelatin
¼ teaspoon blue gel food coloring
2 tablespoons plus 1½ teaspoons strawberry-flavored gelatin
¼ teaspoon pink gel food coloring

1. Divide dough in half; place in separate medium bowls. Let stand at room temperature 15 minutes.

2. Add blue raspberry gelatin and blue food coloring to dough in one bowl. Add strawberry gelatin and pink food coloring to dough in remaining bowl. Beat doughs separately with electric mixer at medium speed until well blended. Form each dough into disc; wrap and refrigerate 1 hour.

3. Roll out blue dough between parchment paper into 10×6-inch rectangle. Repeat with pink dough. Refrigerate both dough rectangles 10 minutes.

4. Place blue dough on top of pink dough. Starting at 10-inch side, roll up into tight log. Wrap and freeze 30 minutes.

5. Preheat oven to 350°F. Grease cookie sheets. Cut log into ¼-inch slices. Place 1 inch apart on prepared cookie sheets. Bake 8 to 10 minutes or until set. Cool on cookie sheets 2 minutes. Remove to wire racks; cool completely. *Makes 40 cookies*

Sour Spirals

Fun & Games

Silly Sunglasses

3½ cups all-purpose flour
½ teaspoon salt
1½ cups sugar
1 cup (2 sticks) unsalted butter, softened
2 eggs
2 teaspoons vanilla
24 to 32 fruit-flavored hard candies, crushed
Assorted colored decorating icings
Assorted decors

1. Whisk flour and salt in medium bowl.

2. Beat sugar and butter in large bowl with electric mixer at medium speed until light and fluffy. Add eggs, 1 at a time, beating until blended after each addition. Add vanilla; beat until blended.

3. Gradually add flour mixture, beating until blended after each addition. Divide dough evenly into 2 discs. Wrap and refrigerate 1 hour.

4. Preheat oven to 350°F. Line cookie sheets with silicone mats or parchment paper. Working with 1 disc at a time, roll out dough between parchment paper to ¼-inch thickness. Cut out sunglasses shapes with sharp knife (approximately 4×2-inch shapes). Place 2 inches apart on prepared cookie sheets. Cut out lenses from sunglasses; discard. Refrigerate 15 minutes.

5. Sprinkle crushed candy into each opening. Bake 10 minutes or until candy is melted and cookies are set. Cool completely on cookie sheets. Decorate sunglasses with decorating icings and decors as desired. *Makes 12 to 16 cookies*

Billiard Balls

3½ cups all-purpose flour
1 teaspoon salt
1½ cups sugar
1 cup (2 sticks) unsalted butter, softened
2 eggs
2 teaspoons vanilla
2 containers (16 ounces each) white or vanilla frosting
Assorted gel food colorings
Black decorating icing

1. Whisk flour and salt in medium bowl. Beat sugar and butter in large bowl with electric mixer at medium speed until light and fluffy. Add eggs, 1 at a time, beating until blended after each addition. Add vanilla; beat until blended.

2. Gradually add flour mixture, beating until blended after each addition. Divide dough evenly into 2 discs. Wrap and refrigerate 1 hour.

3. Preheat oven to 350°F. Line cookie sheets with parchment paper. Working with 1 disc at a time, roll out dough between parchment paper to ⅜-inch thickness. Cut out 18 large circles with 3-inch round cookie cutter. Place 1 inch apart on prepared cookie sheets. Cut out 18 small circles with 1¼-inch round cookie cutter. Place 1 inch apart on separate prepared cookie sheet. Refrigerate 15 minutes.

4. Bake large circles 15 to 17 minutes or until set. Bake small circles 12 to 15 minutes or until set. Cool on cookie sheets 5 minutes. Remove to wire racks; cool completely.

5. Reserve one fourth of frosting. Divide remaining frosting evenly among small bowls and tint with food colorings to make desired colors. For "solids," spread large circles with tinted frosting. Let stand 10 minutes or until set.

6. For "stripes," spread center two thirds of each large circle with tinted frosting. Let stand 10 minutes or until set. Spread remaining one third of each large circle with reserved white frosting. Let stand 10 minutes or until set.

7. Spread small circles with remaining white frosting. Pipe number in center of each white circle using decorating icing. Spread thin layer of frosting on back of small circles and adhere to center of large circles. Let stand 10 minutes or until set. *Makes 1½ dozen cookies*

Billiard Balls

Palm Trees

1 package (about 16 ounces) refrigerated break-apart sugar cookie dough (24 count)
1 container (16 ounces) white or vanilla frosting
Green and brown gel food colorings
Green sparkling sugar
Assorted colored candy-coated sunflower seeds (optional)

1. Let dough stand at room temperature 5 minutes. Line cookie sheets with parchment paper.

2. Preheat oven to 325°F. Roll out dough between parchment paper to ¼-inch thickness. Cut out palm tree shapes with sharp knife (approximately 3×3-inch shapes). Place 2 inches apart on prepared cookie sheets. Refrigerate 15 minutes.

3. Bake 13 to 15 minutes or until set. Cool on cookie sheets 5 minutes. Remove to wire racks; cool completely.

4. Reserve half of frosting in small bowl. Add green food coloring, a few drops at a time, to remaining frosting; stir until evenly colored. Spread leafy part of cookies with green frosting. Sprinkle with sparkling sugar. Add sunflower seeds, if desired. Let stand 10 minutes or until set.

5. Add brown food coloring, a few drops at a time, to reserved frosting. Spread trunks of cookies with brown frosting. Use toothpick to create rough texture. Let stand 10 minutes or until set.

Makes about 16 cookies

Palm Trees

Nothin' but Net

1 package (about 16 ounces) refrigerated sugar cookie dough
1¼ cups all-purpose flour
2 tablespoons powdered sugar
2 tablespoons lemon juice
Orange, white and black decorating icings

1. Let dough stand at room temperature 15 minutes.

2. Combine dough, flour, powdered sugar and lemon juice in large bowl; beat with electric mixer at medium speed until well blended. Divide dough evenly into 2 discs. Wrap and refrigerate at least 2 hours.

3. Preheat oven to 350°F. Lightly grease cookie sheets. Working with 1 disc at a time, roll out dough between parchment paper to ¼-inch thickness. Cut out basketball-in-net shapes. Place 2 inches apart on prepared cookie sheets.

4. Bake 13 to 15 minutes or until edges are lightly browned. Remove to wire racks; cool completely. Decorate with icings.

Makes 1½ dozen cookies

Tip

These cookies are the perfect treats for a sports-themed birthday party. Try serving them with Nutty Footballs (page 144).

Nothin' but Net

Go Fly a Kite Cookies

3½ cups all-purpose flour
1 teaspoon salt
1½ cups sugar
1 cup (2 sticks) unsalted butter, softened
2 eggs
2 teaspoons vanilla
Royal Icing (recipe follows)
Blue and green gel food colorings
Yellow decorating icing

1. Whisk flour and salt in medium bowl. Beat sugar and butter in large bowl with electric mixer at medium speed until light and fluffy. Add eggs, 1 at a time, beating until blended after each addition. Add vanilla; beat until blended. Gradually add flour mixture, beating until blended after each addition. Divide dough evenly into 2 discs. Wrap and refrigerate 1 hour.

2. Preheat oven to 350°F. Line cookie sheets with parchment paper. Working with 1 disc at a time, roll out dough between parchment paper to ⅜-inch thickness. Cut out circles with 3¼-inch round cookie cutter. Place 1 inch apart on prepared cookie sheets. Refrigerate 15 minutes.

3. Bake 15 to 17 minutes or until set. Cool on cookie sheets 5 minutes. Remove to wire racks; cool completely.

4. Prepare Royal Icing. Reserve ¾ cup Royal Icing. Add blue food coloring, a few drops at a time, to remaining icing to create sky blue; stir until evenly colored. Spread cookies with sky blue icing. Let stand 10 minutes or until set.

5. Pipe clouds using ¼ cup reserved white icing. Divide remaining ½ cup white icing into 2 small bowls. Add food coloring, a drop at a time, to each bowl to make dark blue and green icings. Pipe kites using dark blue and green icings. Pipe kite tails using yellow decorating icing. Let stand 10 minutes or until set. *Makes about 1½ dozen cookies*

Royal Icing: Combine 4 cups powdered sugar, 6 tablespoons water and 3 tablespoons meringue powder in medium bowl. Beat with electric mixer at high speed 7 to 10 minutes or until soft peaks form. Cover surface with plastic wrap until needed. Makes about 2 cups.

Go Fly a Kite Cookies

Monogram Cookies

3½ cups all-purpose flour
1 teaspoon salt
1½ cups sugar
1 cup (2 sticks) unsalted butter, softened
2 eggs
2 teaspoons vanilla
Gel food coloring
1 container (16 ounces) white or vanilla frosting
Assorted jumbo nonpareils

1. Whisk flour and salt in medium bowl.

2. Beat sugar and butter in large bowl with electric mixer at medium speed until light and fluffy. Add eggs, 1 at a time, beating until blended after each addition. Add vanilla; beat until blended.

3. Gradually add flour mixture, beating until blended after each addition. Divide dough evenly into 2 discs. Wrap and refrigerate 1 hour.

4. Preheat oven to 350°F. Line cookie sheets with parchment paper. Working with 1 disc at a time, roll out dough between parchment paper to ³⁄₈-inch thickness. Cut out circles with 3-inch fluted round cookie cutter. Place 1 inch apart on prepared cookie sheets. Cut out letters using 1-inch alphabet cookie cutters; discard. Refrigerate 15 minutes.

5. Bake 15 to 17 minutes or until set. Cool on cookie sheets 5 minutes. Remove to wire racks; cool completely.

6. Add food coloring, a few drops at a time, to frosting; stir until evenly colored. Spread cookies with frosting. Decorate with nonpareils as desired. Let stand 10 minutes or until set.

Makes 2 dozen cookies

Monogram Cookies

Nutty Footballs

  2 cups all-purpose flour
  1/4 cup unsweetened cocoa powder
  1 cup (2 sticks) butter, softened
  1/2 cup sugar
  1 egg
  1/2 teaspoon vanilla
  1 cup finely chopped almonds
    Assorted colored decorating icings (optional)
    White decorating icing

1. Combine flour and cocoa in small bowl. Beat butter and sugar in large bowl with electric mixer at medium speed until light and fluffy. Add egg and vanilla; beat until well blended. Gradually add flour mixture, beating until blended after each addition. Add almonds; beat until well blended. Shape dough into disc. Wrap and refrigerate 30 minutes.

2. Preheat oven to 350°F. Lightly grease cookie sheets. Roll out dough between parchment paper to 1/4-inch thickness. Cut out shapes with 2 1/2- to 3-inch football cookie cutter.* Place 2 inches apart on prepared cookie sheets. Refrigerate 15 minutes.

3. Bake 10 to 12 minutes or until set. Cool on cookie sheets 2 minutes. Remove to wire racks; cool completely. Decorate with colored icings, if desired. Pipe white icing onto footballs to resemble laces.   *Makes 2 dozen cookies*

To make football shapes without a cookie cutter, shape 3 tablespoonfuls of dough into ovals. Place 3 inches apart on prepared cookie sheets. Flatten ovals to 1/4-inch thickness; taper ends.

Nutty Footballs

Flip-Flops

1 package (about 16 ounces) refrigerated break-apart sugar cookie dough (24 count)
1 container (16 ounces) white or vanilla frosting
  Assorted gel food colorings
  Red string licorice
  Edible cake decorations*
  Star-shaped candy sprinkles

Edible cake decorations are made from molded sugar. They can be found in the baking aisle at large supermarkets, party supply stores and craft stores.

1. Let dough stand at room temperature 5 minutes. Line cookie sheets with parchment paper.

2. Preheat oven to 325°F. Roll out dough between parchment paper to ¼-inch thickness. Cut out flip-flop shapes with sharp knife (approximately 3×1½-inch shapes). Place 2 inches apart on prepared cookie sheets. Refrigerate 15 minutes.

3. Bake 13 to 15 minutes or until set. Cool on cookie sheets 5 minutes. Remove to wire racks; cool completely.

4. Divide frosting evenly among small bowls and tint with food colorings to make desired colors. Spread cookies with frosting. Cut licorice for straps; press into frosting. Top with cake decorations. Decorate with candy sprinkles as desired. Let stand 10 minutes or until set.

Makes about 20 cookies

Tip

Flip-flops come in hundreds of colors and designs, so feel free to experiment with frosting colors, fun stripes or swirls in the frosting or even other kinds of sprinkles and candies to make pretty patterns.

Flip-Flops

Favorite Foods

Mighty Milkshakes

1 package (about 19 ounces) brownie mix, plus ingredients to prepare mix
1 package (14 ounces) milk chocolate or peanut butter candy discs
½ (16-ounce) container white or vanilla frosting
    Colored drinking straws
    Colored sprinkles

1. Preheat oven to 350°F. Coat 9-inch square baking pan with nonstick cooking spray.

2. Prepare brownie mix according to package directions; pour batter into prepared pan. Bake 35 minutes or until toothpick inserted into center comes out clean. Cool completely in pan on wire rack. Cover; freeze 1 hour or overnight.

3. Run knife around edges of brownies. Place cutting board over baking pan; invert and let stand until brownies release from pan. Trim edges; discard. Cut into 18 rectangles.

4. Microwave candy discs in medium microwavable bowl on HIGH 1 minute. Stir. Microwave at additional 15-second intervals until smooth and spreadable. Stand brownies up on small side. Spread all sides except bottom of brownies with candy mixture. Let stand on wire racks 10 minutes or until set.

5. Pipe frosting on top of each brownie for whipped cream. Decorate with straws and sprinkles.   *Makes 1½ dozen brownies*

Over Easy Cookies

1 package (about 16 ounces) refrigerated break-apart sugar cookie dough (24 count)
1 package (14 ounces) white chocolate candy discs
   Yellow gel food coloring
1 cup prepared white or vanilla frosting

1. Let dough stand at room temperature 5 minutes. Line cookie sheets with parchment paper.

2. Preheat oven to 325°F. Roll out dough between parchment paper to $\frac{1}{4}$-inch thickness. Cut out egg white shapes with sharp knife (approximately $2\frac{1}{2} \times 3\frac{1}{2}$-inch shapes). Place egg whites 2 inches apart on prepared cookie sheets. Cut out yolks with $1\frac{1}{4}$-inch round cookie cutter. Place egg yolks 1 inch apart on separate prepared cookie sheet. Refrigerate 15 minutes.

3. Bake egg whites 15 to 17 minutes or until set. Bake egg yolks 10 to 12 minutes or until set. Cool on cookie sheets 5 minutes. Remove to wire racks; cool completely.

4. Microwave candy discs in medium microwavable bowl on HIGH 1 minute. Stir. Microwave at additional 15-second intervals until smooth and spreadable. Spread egg whites with candy mixture. Let stand on wire racks 10 minutes or until set.

5. Add food coloring, a few drops at a time, to frosting; stir until evenly colored. Spread egg yolks with yellow frosting. Spread thin layer of frosting on back of egg yolks and adhere to egg whites. Let stand 10 minutes or until set.

Makes about 1 dozen cookies

Over Easy Cookies, Makin' Bacon Cookies (page 160)

Marshmallow Ice Cream Cone Cookies

1 package (about 16 ounces) refrigerated sugar cookie dough
6 ice cream sugar cones, broken into pieces
1 container (16 ounces) white frosting
1 package (about 10 ounces) colored miniature marshmallows
Colored sprinkles

1. Let dough stand at room temperature 15 minutes.

2. Preheat oven to 350°F. Place sugar cones in food processor. Process using on/off pulsing action until finely ground. Combine dough and sugar cones in large bowl; beat until well blended.

3. Shape dough into 3 equal balls. Pat each ball into 9-inch circle on lightly floured surface. Cut each circle into 6 wedges; place 2 inches apart on ungreased cookie sheets.

4. Bake 10 to 11 minutes or until edges are lightly browned. While cookies are still warm, score crisscross pattern into cookies. Cool on cookie sheets 5 minutes. Remove cookies to wire racks; cool completely.

5. Spread 2-inch strip of frosting at wide end of each cookie. Press marshmallows into frosting; top with sprinkles.

Makes 1½ dozen cookies

Marshmallow Ice Cream Cone Cookies

Peanut Butter & Jelly Sandwich Cookies

1 package (about 16 ounces) refrigerated sugar cookie dough
1 tablespoon unsweetened cocoa powder
¾ cup creamy peanut butter
½ cup grape jelly

1. Reserve three fourths of dough; wrap and refrigerate. Beat remaining one fourth of dough and cocoa in small bowl with electric mixer at medium speed until well blended; cover and refrigerate.

2. Shape reserved dough into 5½-inch log. Roll out chocolate dough between parchment paper into 9½×6½-inch rectangle. Place log in center of rectangle.

3. Bring chocolate dough up and over log so log is wrapped in chocolate dough; press edges to seal. Flatten top and sides of dough slightly to form square. Wrap and freeze 10 minutes.

4. Preheat oven to 350°F. Cut dough into ¼-inch slices. Place 2 inches apart on ungreased cookie sheets. Reshape dough edges into square, if necessary. Press edge of dough slightly to form indentation so dough resembles slice of bread.

5. Bake 8 to 11 minutes or until lightly browned. Immediately straighten cookie edges with spatula. Cool on cookie sheets 2 minutes. Remove to wire racks; cool completely.

6. Spread peanut butter on half of cookies. Spread jelly over peanut butter; top with remaining cookies, pressing gently.

Makes 11 sandwich cookies

Peanut Butter & Jelly Sandwich Cookies

Cupcake Cookies

3½ cups all-purpose flour
1 teaspoon salt
1½ cups sugar
1 cup (2 sticks) unsalted butter, softened
2 eggs
2 teaspoons vanilla
1½ containers (16 ounces each) white or vanilla frosting
   Assorted gel food colorings
   Large confetti sprinkles

1. Whisk flour and salt in medium bowl.

2. Beat sugar and butter in large bowl with electric mixer at medium speed until light and fluffy. Add eggs, 1 at a time, beating until blended after each addition. Add vanilla; beat until blended.

3. Gradually add flour mixture, beating until blended after each addition. Divide dough evenly into 2 discs. Wrap and refrigerate 1 hour.

4. Preheat oven to 350°F. Line cookie sheets with parchment paper. Working with 1 disc at a time, roll out dough between parchment paper to ⅜-inch thickness. Cut out cupcake shapes with sharp knife (approximately 2½×2½-inch shapes). Place 1 inch apart on prepared cookie sheets. Refrigerate 15 minutes.

5. Bake 15 to 17 minutes or until set. Cool on cookie sheets 5 minutes. Remove to wire racks; cool completely.

6. Reserve half of frosting. Add food coloring, a few drops at a time, to remaining half of frosting; stir until evenly colored. Spread bottom half of cookies with frosting. Let stand 3 minutes or until just beginning to set. Press toothpick into frosting to create lines that resemble paper liner cups. Let stand on wire racks 10 minutes or until set.

7. Add food coloring, a few drops at a time, to reserved frosting; stir until evenly colored. (Divide frosting before adding food coloring if more colors are desired.) Spread top half of cookies with frosting. Press sprinkles into frosting. Let stand 10 minutes or until set.

Makes 2 dozen cookies

Cupcake Cookies

Watermelon Slices

2 packages (about 16 ounces each) refrigerated sugar cookie dough
½ cup all-purpose flour, divided
Green and red food colorings
Mini chocolate chips

1. Let doughs stand at room temperature 15 minutes.

2. Combine 1 package dough, ¼ cup flour and green food coloring in large bowl; beat with electric mixer at medium speed until well blended. Wrap and refrigerate 2 hours.

3. Combine remaining package dough, remaining ¼ cup flour and red food coloring in separate large bowl; beat at medium speed until well blended. Shape into 9-inch-long log. Wrap and refrigerate 2 hours.

4. Roll out green dough between parchment paper into 9×8-inch rectangle. Place log in center of green rectangle. Fold edges up and around log; press edges to seal. Roll gently to form smooth log. Wrap and freeze 30 minutes.

5. Preheat oven to 350°F. Cut log into ⅜-inch-thick slices. Cut each slice in half. Place 2 inches apart on ungreased cookie sheets. Gently reshape, if necessary. Press several mini chocolate chips into each slice for watermelon seeds.

6. Bake 8 to 11 minutes or until set. Cool on cookie sheets 1 minute. Remove to wire racks; cool completely.

Makes about 4 dozen cookies

Watermelon Slices

Makin' Bacon Cookies

1 package (about 16 ounces) refrigerated break-apart sugar cookie dough (24 count)
½ cup water, divided
Red, brown and yellow gel food colorings

1. Let dough stand at room temperature 5 minutes. Line cookie sheets with parchment paper.

2. Preheat oven to 325°F. Roll out dough between parchment paper to ¼-inch thickness. Cut out bacon shapes with sharp knife (approximately 1×3½-inch shapes). Place 2 inches apart on prepared cookie sheets. Refrigerate 15 minutes.

3. Bake 13 to 15 minutes or until set. Cool on cookie sheets 5 minutes. Remove to wire racks; cool completely.

4. Place ¼ cup water in small bowl. Add a few drops of red and brown food colorings; stir until evenly colored. Place remaining ¼ cup water in another small bowl. Add a few drops of red and yellow food colorings; stir until evenly colored. Paint cookies to resemble bacon with small clean paintbrushes,* using as little water as possible for color to saturate. Leave some areas unpainted to resemble bacon fat. Let stand 1 hour or until dry.

Makes about 2 dozen cookies

*Do not use paintbrushes that have been used for anything other than food.

Makin' Bacon Cookies

Burger Bliss

Buns

    1 package (about 16 ounces) refrigerated sugar cookie dough
    ½ cup creamy peanut butter
    ⅓ cup all-purpose flour
    ¼ cup packed brown sugar
    ½ teaspoon vanilla
    Beaten egg white and sesame seeds (optional)

Burgers

    ½ (16-ounce) package refrigerated sugar cookie dough*
    3 tablespoons unsweetened cocoa powder
    2 tablespoons packed brown sugar
    ½ teaspoon vanilla
    Red, yellow and green decorating icings

Reserve remaining dough for another use.

1. Preheat oven to 350°F. Grease cookie sheets.

2. For buns, let 1 package dough stand at room temperature 15 minutes. Combine dough, peanut butter, flour, ¼ cup brown sugar and ½ teaspoon vanilla in large bowl; beat with electric mixer at medium speed until well blended. Shape into 48 (1-inch) balls; place 2 inches apart on prepared cookie sheets.

3. Bake 14 minutes or until lightly browned. Brush half of cookies with egg white and sprinkle with sesame seeds after 10 minutes, if desired. Cool on cookie sheets 2 minutes. Remove to wire racks; cool completely.

4. For burgers, let ½ package dough stand at room temperature 15 minutes. Combine dough, cocoa, 2 tablespoons brown sugar and ½ teaspoon vanilla in medium bowl; beat with electric mixer at medium speed until well blended. Shape into 24 (1-inch) balls; place 2 inches apart on prepared cookie sheets. Flatten to ¼-inch thickness.

5. Bake 12 minutes or until set. Cool on cookie sheets 2 minutes. Remove to wire racks; cool completely. To assemble, use icing to attach burgers to flat sides of 24 buns. Pipe red, yellow and green icings on burgers. Top with remaining buns. *Makes 2 dozen sandwich cookies*

Burger Bliss

Citrus Slices

1 package (about 16 ounces) refrigerated sugar cookie dough
3 tablespoons all-purpose flour
$\frac{1}{2}$ teaspoon lemon extract
   Yellow, green and orange food colorings
1 egg white, lightly beaten
   Yellow, green and orange decorating sugars
$\frac{1}{2}$ teaspoon lime extract
$\frac{1}{2}$ teaspoon orange extract
   Coarse white decorating sugar

1. Let dough stand at room temperature 15 minutes.

2. Combine dough and flour in large bowl; beat with electric mixer at medium speed until well blended. Divide dough into 3 equal pieces.

3. Add lemon extract and yellow food coloring to 1 dough piece in medium bowl; beat until well blended. Shape dough into 6×1½-inch log; flatten 1 side of log to make half-moon shape. Brush rounded side of log with egg white; sprinkle with yellow sugar until evenly coated. Wrap and freeze 1 hour.

4. Repeat step 3 with second piece of dough, lime extract, green food coloring and green sugar.

5. Repeat step 3 with remaining piece of dough, orange extract, orange food coloring and orange sugar.

6. Preheat oven to 350°F. Lightly grease cookie sheets. Cut logs into ¼-inch slices; place 2 inches apart on prepared cookie sheets. Sprinkle with coarse white sugar.

7. Bake 9 to 11 minutes or until set. Immediately score hot cookies. Cool on cookie sheets 2 minutes. Remove to wire racks; cool completely. *Makes 6 dozen cookies*

Citrus Slices

Cupcake Cuties

Hedgehogs

1 package (about 15 ounces) chocolate cake mix, plus ingredients to prepare mix
1 container (16 ounces) chocolate frosting
  Black jelly beans
  Small round white candies
  Black decorating gel
  Candy-coated licorice pieces

1. Preheat oven to 350°F. Place 22 standard (2-inch) silicone muffin cups on large baking sheet or line 22 standard (2½-inch) muffin cups with paper baking cups.

2. Prepare cake mix according to package directions. Spoon batter into prepared muffin cups, filling two-thirds full. Bake 18 to 22 minutes or until toothpick inserted into centers comes out clean. If using muffin pans, cool cupcakes in pans 10 minutes; remove to wire racks to cool completely.

3. Frost cupcakes. Cut jelly beans in half crosswise for noses. Arrange jelly bean halves and round candies on one side of each cupcake to create faces; add dot of decorating gel to each eye. Arrange licorice pieces around face and all over each cupcake.

Makes 22 cupcakes

Colorful Caterpillar Cupcakes

  1 package (about 15 ounces) vanilla cake mix
1¼ cups water
  3 eggs
  ⅓ cup vegetable oil
     Food coloring
  1 container (16 ounces) vanilla frosting
     Assorted candies, candy-coated chocolate pieces, red string licorice and lollipops
     Multi-colored gummy worms

1. Preheat oven to 350°F. Line 22 standard (2½-inch) muffin cups with paper baking cups.*

2. Beat cake mix, water, eggs and oil in large bowl with electric mixer at low speed 30 seconds. Beat at medium speed 2 minutes or until well blended. Divide batter between 5 bowls; tint each bowl with different color food coloring. Spoon batter into prepared muffin cups, filling two-thirds full.

3. Bake 18 to 22 minutes or until toothpick inserted into centers comes out clean. Cool cupcakes in pans 10 minutes; remove to wire racks to cool completely.

4. Set aside 2 cupcakes for caterpillar head. Frost remaining cupcakes. Place 1 cupcake on its side towards one end of serving platter. Place second cupcake on its side next to first cupcake; arrange remaining cupcakes, alternating colors, in row to create body of caterpillar.

5. Frost 1 reserved cupcake; decorate with assorted candies, licorice and lollipops to create face and antennae. Place plain cupcake upright at front of cupcake row for head; top with face cupcake on its side. Cut gummy worms into small pieces; attach to caterpillar body with frosting to create legs. *Makes 22 cupcakes*

Use white paper baking cups to best show colors of caterpillar.

Colorful Caterpillar Cupcakes

Dinocakes

1 package (about 15 ounces) chocolate fudge or devil's food cake mix, plus ingredients to prepare mix
44 long chewy chocolate candies (3×¼ inch), divided
10 to 15 small chewy chocolate candies
1 container (16 ounces) chocolate frosting
Candy sprinkles and decorating decors

1. Preheat oven to 350°F. Line 22 standard (2½-inch) muffin cups with paper baking cups.

2. Prepare cake mix according to package directions. Spoon batter into prepared muffin cups, filling two-thirds full. Bake 18 to 22 minutes or until toothpick inserted into centers comes out clean. Cool cupcakes in pans 10 minutes; remove to wire racks to cool completely.

3. Shape 22 long candies into dinosaur heads. (If candies are too stiff to bend, microwave on LOW (30%) for 6 to 8 seconds to soften.)

4. Cut about 1 inch from remaining 22 long candies with scissors; shape each into pointed tail. Make 4 to 5 small cuts along length of candies, being careful not to cut all the way through. Curve candies into tail shape. Press and flatten small candies into rectangles; cut rectangles into small triangles for dinosaur spikes.

5. Frost cupcakes. Press candy head and tail into opposite sides of each cupcake; arrange candy triangles in between. Decorate with sprinkles; press decors into dinosaur heads for eyes.

Makes 22 cupcakes

Dinocakes

Little Lamb Cakes

    1 package (about 15 ounces) yellow cake mix, plus ingredients to prepare mix
    1 container (16 ounces) vanilla frosting
  15 large marshmallows
     Pink jelly beans or decorating candies
    1 package (10½ ounces) mini marshmallows
     Black string licorice
  44 mini chocolate chips

1. Preheat oven to 350°F. Line 22 standard (2½-inch) muffin cups with paper baking cups.

2. Prepare cake mix according to package directions. Spoon batter into prepared muffin cups, filling two-thirds full. Bake 18 to 22 minutes or until toothpick inserted into centers comes out clean. Cool cupcakes in pans 10 minutes; remove to wire racks to cool completely.

3. Frost cupcakes. Cut each large marshmallow crosswise into 3 pieces. Stretch pieces into oval shapes; arrange on cupcakes to create ears. Attach pink jelly bean to each ear with frosting.

4. Press mini marshmallows into frosting around edges of cupcakes. Cut jelly beans in half crosswise; cut licorice into ½-inch pieces. Arrange chocolate chips, jelly bean halves and licorice pieces on each cupcake to create faces.

Makes 22 cupcakes

Little Lamb Cakes

Miss Pinky the Pig Cupcakes

2 jars (10 ounces each) maraschino cherries, well drained
1 package (about 15 ounces) white cake mix *without* pudding in the mix
1 cup sour cream
½ cup vegetable oil
3 egg whites
¼ cup water
½ teaspoon almond extract
   Red food coloring
1 container (16 ounces) cream cheese frosting
48 small gumdrops
   White decorating icing, mini candy-coated chocolate pieces, mini chocolate chips
      and red sugar

1. Preheat oven to 350°F. Line 24 standard (2½-inch) muffin cups with paper baking cups. Spray 24 mini (1¾-inch) muffin cups with nonstick cooking spray. Pat cherries dry with paper towels. Place in food processor; process 4 to 5 seconds or until finely chopped.

2. Beat cake mix, sour cream, oil, egg whites, water and almond extract in large bowl with electric mixer at low speed about 1 minute or until blended. Beat at medium speed 1 to 2 minutes or until smooth. Stir in cherries.

3. Spoon 2 slightly rounded tablespoons batter into each standard muffin cup, filling about half full. (Cups will be slightly less full than normal.) Spoon remaining batter into prepared mini muffin cups, filling each about one-third full.

4. Bake standard cupcakes 14 to 18 minutes and mini cupcakes 7 to 9 minutes or until toothpick inserted into centers comes out clean. Cool cupcakes in pans 5 minutes; remove to wire racks to cool completely.

5. Add food coloring to frosting in small bowl, a few drops at a time, until desired shade of pink is reached. Frost standard cupcakes. Place mini cupcakes, upside down, off center of each standard cupcake. Frost mini cupcakes.

6. Place gumdrops between two layers of waxed paper. Flatten to ⅛-inch thickness with rolling pin; cut out triangles for ears. Use icing and chocolate pieces for eyes; create nose with chocolate chips and sugar.

Makes 24 cupcakes

Miss Pinky the Pig Cupcakes

Mini Mice

1 package (about 15 ounces) chocolate cake mix, plus ingredients to prepare mix
1 container (16 ounces) chocolate frosting
1 cup white frosting (optional)
   Small black and pink hard candies or decors
   Small fruit-flavored pastel candy wafers
   Black string licorice

1. Preheat oven to 350°F. Line 48 mini (1¾-inch) muffin cups with paper baking cups.

2. Prepare cake mix according to package directions. Spoon batter into prepared muffin cups, filling almost full. Bake about 12 minutes or until toothpick inserted into centers comes out clean. Cool cupcakes in pans 10 minutes; remove to wire racks to cool completely.

3. For brown mice, frost cupcakes with chocolate frosting; use knife or small spatula to pull up frosting and create fuzzy appearance. For speckled mice, frost cupcakes with white frosting; use toothpick to add streaks of chocolate frosting.

4. Arrange candies on one side of each cupcake to create eyes, nose and ears. Cut licorice into 3-inch lengths; press into opposite end of each cupcake to create tail.

Makes about 60 mini cupcakes

Cupcakes can be baked in advance and frozen, undecorated, in an airtight container for up to three months. Defrost them at room temperature for several hours.

Mini Mice

Panda Cupcakes

1 package (about 15 ounces) yellow cake mix, plus ingredients to prepare mix
1 container (16 ounces) vanilla frosting
44 large chocolate nonpareil candies or chocolate discs*
44 small chocolate nonpareil candies
8 ounces semisweet chocolate, chopped *or* 1½ cups semisweet chocolate chips
44 white candy sprinkles or decors
22 red jelly beans

Chocolate discs are available at many gourmet, craft and baking supply stores.

1. Preheat oven to 350°F. Line 22 standard (2½-inch) muffin cups with paper baking cups.

2. Prepare cake mix according to package directions. Spoon batter into prepared muffin cups, filling two-thirds full. Bake 18 to 22 minutes or until toothpick inserted into centers comes out clean. Cool cupcakes in pans 10 minutes; remove to wire racks to cool completely.

3. Frost cupcakes. Arrange 2 chocolate discs on edge of each cupcake to create ears. Attach 1 nonpareil candy to each ear with frosting.

4. Place semisweet chocolate in small food storage bag. Microwave on HIGH about 1½ minutes or until chocolate is melted, kneading bag every 30 seconds. Cut small hole in corner of bag; pipe kidney shapes on cupcakes for eyes. Place candy sprinkle on each eye. Place jelly bean between eyes for nose; pipe mouth with melted chocolate.   *Makes 22 cupcakes*

Panda Cupcakes

Chocolate Moose

1 package (about 15 ounces) chocolate cake mix, plus ingredients to prepare mix
1 container (16 ounces) milk chocolate frosting
½ to ¾ cup vanilla frosting
1 package (12 ounces) semisweet chocolate chips
2 tablespoons shortening
White round candies
Small black candies
Black decorating gel
Pretzel twists

1. Preheat oven to 350°F. Line 22 standard (2½-inch) muffin cups with paper baking cups.

2. Prepare cake mix according to package directions. Spoon batter into prepared muffin cups, filling two-thirds full. Bake 18 to 22 minutes or until toothpick inserted into centers comes out clean. Cool cupcakes in pans 10 minutes; remove to wire racks to cool completely.

3. Combine chocolate frosting and ½ cup vanilla frosting in medium bowl until well blended. (Stir in additional vanilla frosting if lighter color is desired.) Frost cupcakes.

4. Place chocolate chips and shortening in medium microwavable bowl. Microwave on HIGH 1½ minutes or until chocolate is melted and mixture is smooth, stirring every 30 seconds. Place chocolate in pastry bag or small food storage bag with small corner cut off. Pipe chocolate mixture into shape of moose head on each cupcake as shown in photo; smooth chocolate with small spatula. (Chocolate may need to be reheated slightly if it becomes too stiff to pipe.)

5. Arrange candies on cupcakes to create eyes and noses; add dot of decorating gel or chocolate mixture to each eye. Break off small section of each pretzel twist to form antlers. Push ends of pretzels into top of cupcakes.   *Makes 22 cupcakes*

Chocolate Moose

Butterfly Cupcakes

1 package (about 15 ounces) cake mix, any flavor, plus ingredients to prepare mix
1 container (16 ounces) vanilla frosting
  Blue and green food coloring
  Colored sugar
  Candy-coated chocolate pieces
  Red string licorice, cut into 4-inch pieces

1. Preheat oven to 350°F. Lightly spray 22 standard (2½-inch) muffin cups with nonstick cooking spray.

2. Prepare cake mix according to package directions. Spoon batter into prepared muffin cups, filling two-thirds full. Bake 18 to 22 minutes or until toothpick inserted into centers comes out clean. Cool cupcakes in pans 10 minutes; remove to wire racks to cool completely

3. Divide frosting between 2 small bowls. Add one color food coloring to each bowl, a few drops at a time, until desired shades of blue and green are reached.

4. Cut cupcakes in half vertically. Place halves together, cut sides out, to resemble butterfly wings. Frost cupcakes; decorate with colored sugar and chocolate pieces. Snip each end of licorice pieces for antennae; place in center of each cupcake.   *Makes 22 cupcakes*

Butterfly Cupcakes

Tempting Turtles

1 package (about 15 ounces) chocolate cake mix, plus ingredients to prepare mix
1½ packages (12 ounces each) small chewy chocolate candies
    Green food coloring
1 container (16 ounces) vanilla frosting
    Chocolate-covered raisins, chocolate chips or candy-coated chocolate pieces
    White decorating decors

1. Preheat oven to 350°F. Line 22 standard (2½-inch) muffin cups with paper baking cups or spray with nonstick cooking spray.

2. Prepare cake mix according to package directions. Spoon batter into prepared muffin cups, filling two-thirds full. Bake 18 to 22 minutes or until toothpick inserted into centers comes out clean. Cool cupcakes in pans 10 minutes; remove to wire racks to cool completely.

3. For each turtle, cut 2 candies in half; flatten slightly and shape pieces into feet. Shape 1 candy into turtle head. (To soften candies for easier shaping, microwave on LOW (30%) 6 to 8 seconds.) Stretch 1 candy into long thin rope; cut into ½-inch pieces for tails.

4. Remove paper baking cups; cut off ½ inch from bottom of each cupcake. Add food coloring to frosting in medium bowl, a few drops at a time, until desired shade of green is reached. Frost cupcakes.

5. Press candy head and tail into opposite ends of each cupcake; press chocolate-covered raisins into frosting. Press decors into head for eyes. Arrange 4 candy feet around each turtle.

Makes 22 cupcakes

Tempting Turtles

Monkey A-Rounds

    1 package (about 15 ounces) chocolate cake mix, plus ingredients to prepare mix
    1 container (16 ounces) chocolate frosting
    1 container (16 ounces) vanilla frosting
      Yellow food coloring
  44 chocolate discs
      Small black jelly beans
      Black string licorice

1. Preheat oven to 350°F. Line 22 standard (2½-inch) muffin cups with paper baking cups.

2. Prepare cake mix according to package directions. Spoon batter into prepared muffin cups, filling two-thirds full. Bake 18 to 22 minutes or until toothpick inserted into centers comes out clean. Cool cupcakes in pans 10 minutes; remove to wire racks to cool completely.

3. Frost cupcakes with chocolate frosting. Place white frosting in small bowl. Add food coloring, a few drops at a time, until desired shade of yellow is reached. Transfer frosting to pastry bag or small food storage bag with small corner cut off.

4. Pipe circle of yellow frosting in center of each chocolate disc for ears. Cut jelly beans in half crosswise for eyes; cut licorice into smaller lengths for mouths and noses. Pipe yellow frosting into oval shape on each cupcake as shown in photo; arrange eyes just above oval and ears on either side of cupcake. Arrange licorice noses and mouths inside oval. Use toothpick or knife to pull up frosting at top of cupcake into hair (or use pastry bag with special tip to pipe hair). *Makes 22 cupcakes*

Monkey A-Rounds

Fishy Friends

1 package (about 15 ounces) cake mix, any flavor, plus ingredients to prepare mix
1 container (16 ounces) vanilla frosting
 Orange, purple and blue food coloring
 Assorted color jelly candy fruit slices
 Colored round gummy candies
 White round candies
 Black decorating gel

1. Preheat oven to 350°F. Line 22 standard (2½-inch) muffin cups with paper baking cups.

2. Prepare cake mix according to package directions. Spoon batter into prepared muffin cups, filling two-thirds full. Bake 18 to 22 minutes or until toothpick inserted into centers comes out clean. Cool cupcakes in pans 10 minutes; remove to wire racks to cool completely.

3. Divide frosting between 3 small bowls. Add food coloring, a few drops at a time, until desired shades are reached. Frost cupcakes.

4. Cut jelly candies into triangles for fins and tails. Arrange white candies and gummy candies at one end of each cupcake to create faces; add dot of decorating gel to each eye. Arrange jelly candy triangles on top and side of each cupcake.   *Makes 22 cupcakes*

Fishy Friends

Princess Power

Fairy Tale Cupcakes

1 package (about 15 ounces) cake mix, any flavor, plus ingredients to prepare mix
1 container (16 ounces) vanilla frosting
  Pink, purple , blue and yellow food coloring
  Silver dragees
  Assorted decoratifs and decors

1. Preheat oven to 350°F. Line 22 standard (2½-inch) muffin cups with paper baking cups or spray with nonstick cooking spray.

2. Prepare cake mix according to package directions. Spoon batter into prepared muffin cups, filling two-thirds full. Bake 18 to 22 minutes or until toothpick inserted into centers comes out clean. Cool cupcakes in pans 10 minutes; remove to wire racks to cool completely.

3. Divide frosting between 4 bowls; add different food coloring to each bowl, a few drops at a time, until desired shades are reached. Frost cupcakes with pink, purple and blue frosting; smooth tops with small spatula.

4. Spoon yellow frosting into pastry bag with round decorating tip or small food storage bag with small corner cut off. Pipe crowns and wands on cupcakes; decorate with dragees, decoratifs and decors.

Makes 22 cupcakes

Marshmallow Delights

       2 cups all-purpose flour
       1 teaspoon baking soda
       1 teaspoon baking powder
    $\frac{1}{2}$ teaspoon salt
    $\frac{1}{2}$ cup sour cream
    $\frac{1}{2}$ cup milk
       1 teaspoon vanilla
       1 cup granulated sugar
    $\frac{1}{2}$ cup (1 stick) butter, softened
       2 eggs
         Green food coloring
    $1\frac{1}{2}$ cups vanilla frosting
       3 cups fruit-flavored mini marshmallows
         Green sparkling sugar

1. Preheat oven to 350°F. Line 12 standard (2½-inch) muffin cups with paper baking cups. Sift flour, baking soda, baking powder and salt into medium bowl. Combine sour cream, milk and vanilla in small bowl until well blended.

2. Beat granulated sugar and butter in large bowl with electric mixer at medium speed 2 minutes or until fluffy. Add eggs, 1 at a time, beating well after each addition. Add flour mixture alternately with sour cream mixture, beginning and ending with flour mixture, beating well after each addition. Spoon batter evenly into prepared muffin cups.

3. Bake 21 to 23 minutes or until toothpick inserted into centers comes out clean. Cool cupcakes in pan 5 minutes; remove to wire rack to cool completely.

4. Add food coloring to frosting in small bowl, a few drops at a time, until desired shade of green is reached. Frost cupcakes. Arrange marshmallows over frosting; sprinkle with sparkling sugar.

Makes 12 cupcakes

Marshmallow Delights

Little Princesses

1 package (about 15 ounces) cake mix, any flavor, plus ingredients to prepare mix
2 containers (16 ounces each) vanilla frosting
Pink, green and purple food coloring
12 mini doll picks* or 4- to 5-inch dolls
Assorted jumbo nonpareils

*Mini doll picks can be found in packages of 4 at craft stores with the cake decorating supplies.

1. Preheat oven to 350°F. Grease 24 standard (2½-inch) muffin cups. Prepare cake mix according to package directions. Spoon batter into prepared muffin cups, filling two-thirds full. Bake 18 to 20 minutes or until toothpick inserted into centers comes out clean. Cool cupcakes in pans 10 minutes; remove to wire racks to cool completely.

2. Cut off rounded tops of cupcakes with serrated knife; discard scraps. Place half of cupcakes upside down on parchment paper-lined tray or baking sheet. Spread thin layer of frosting on cupcakes. Top with remaining cupcakes, upside down. Insert doll pick into top of each cupcake stack. Trim sides of each top cupcake with serrated knife, cutting at slight angle from top to bottom, working around cupcake to create bell shape (doll's skirt). Top of cupcake should be just as wide as base of doll torso.

3. Spread thin layer of frosting over cupcakes with small offset spatula, being careful not to rip cupcake. (Frosting does not need to be completely smooth at this point, but should cover everything from doll's waist down to parchment paper.) Freeze 10 minutes to set frosting.

4. Divide remaining frosting between 3 bowls; add different food coloring to each bowl, a few drops at a time, until desired shades are reached. Frost cupcakes, completely covering first layer of frosting. Make vertical waves through frosting with mini spatula, starting in back and working around cupcake. Freeze 10 minutes to set frosting.

5. Spoon frosting into piping bags with round decorating tip or small food storage bags with small corner cut off. Pipe shirts on dolls; smooth with spatula or finger. Pipe border around dolls' waists to cover seam between shirt and skirt. Transfer to serving plates or large tray. Pipe border around bottom of cupcakes. Pipe flowers on skirts; press nonpareil into center of each flower. *Makes 12 mini cakes*

Tip: If using dolls rather than doll picks, remove the dolls' clothing and wrap the hair in plastic wrap to keep it clean while decorating.

Little Princesses

Angelic Cupcakes

    1 package (about 16 ounces) angel food cake mix
1¼ cups cold water
 ¼ teaspoon peppermint extract (optional)
    Red food coloring
4½ cups whipped topping

1. Preheat oven to 375°F. Line 36 standard (2½-inch) muffin cups with paper baking cups.

2. Beat cake mix, water and peppermint extract, if desired, in large bowl with electric mixer at low speed 2 minutes. Pour half of batter into medium bowl; fold in 9 drops food coloring. Alternate spoonfuls of white and pink batter in each prepared muffin cup, filling three-fourths full.

3. Bake 11 minutes or until cupcakes are golden brown with deep cracks on top. Remove to wire racks to cool completely.

4. Divide whipped topping between two small bowls. Add 2 drops food coloring to 1 bowl; stir gently until whipped topping is evenly colored. Frost cupcakes with pink and white whipped topping.

Makes 36 cupcakes

Tip

Pink food coloring is available at specialty baking and craft stores; it can be used instead of red. You may need to add more than the recipe directs to reach the desired shade of pink.

Angelic Cupcakes

Friendly Frogs

1 package (about 15 ounces) cake mix, any flavor, plus ingredients to prepare mix
  Green food coloring
1 container (16 ounces) vanilla frosting
  Green sparkling sugar (optional)
  Black round candies or candy-coated chocolate pieces
  White chocolate candy discs
  Black and red string licorice
  Green jelly candy fruit slices (optional)

1. Preheat oven to 350°F. Line 22 standard (2½-inch) muffin cups with paper baking cups.

2. Prepare cake mix according to package directions. Spoon batter into prepared muffin cups, filling two-thirds full. Bake 18 to 22 minutes or until toothpick inserted into centers comes out clean. Cool cupcakes in pans 10 minutes; remove to wire racks to cool completely.

3. Add food coloring to frosting in small bowl, a few drops at a time, until desired shade of green is reached. Frost cupcakes; sprinkle with sparkling sugar, if desired.

4. Use small dab of frosting to attach black candies to white discs for eyes. Cut licorice into smaller lengths for mouths and noses. Arrange candies on cupcakes to create frog faces.

5. Use scissors to cut jelly candies into feet, if desired. Set cupcakes on candy feet when ready to serve. *Makes 22 cupcakes*

Friendly Frogs

Under the Sea

1 package (about 15 ounces) cake mix, any flavor, plus ingredients to prepare mix
2 containers (16 ounces each) vanilla frosting
   Blue, green, yellow, red and purple food coloring
   White sparkling sugar (optional)
   Black decorating gel
   Assorted color decors, nonpareils and candy fish

1. Preheat oven to 350°F. Line 22 standard (2½-inch) muffin cups with paper baking cups or spray with nonstick cooking spray.

2. Prepare cake mix according to package directions. Spoon batter into prepared muffin cups, filling two-thirds full. Bake 18 to 22 minutes or until toothpick inserted into centers comes out clean. Cool cupcakes in pans 10 minutes; remove to wire racks to cool completely.

3. Place 1 container frosting in small bowl; add blue and green food coloring, a few drops at a time, until desired shade of aqua is reached. Spoon into pastry bag with large star decorating tip. Pipe aqua frosting in swirl pattern on cupcakes. Sprinkle with sparkling sugar, if desired.

4. Divide remaining frosting between 4 bowls; add different food coloring (except blue) to each bowl, a few drops at a time, until desired shades are reached. Spoon each color into pastry bags with round decorating tip or small food storage bags with small corner cut off. Pipe sea creatures and plants on cupcakes: yellow fish, red lobsters, purple starfish and green seaweed. Decorate with decorating gel, decors and candies.

Makes 22 cupcakes

Under the Sea

Pretty in Pink

 2 cups all-purpose flour
 1 teaspoon baking soda
 1 teaspoon baking powder
 $\frac{1}{2}$ teaspoon salt
 $\frac{1}{2}$ cup sour cream
 $\frac{1}{2}$ cup milk
 1 teaspoon vanilla
 1 cup granulated sugar
 $\frac{1}{2}$ cup (1 stick) butter, softened
 2 eggs
 2 to 3 tablespoons multi-colored cake decors (sprinkles)
   Pink food coloring
 1 container (16 ounces) vanilla frosting
12 small tiaras
   White and pink sparkling sugars

1. Preheat oven to 350°F. Line 12 standard (2½-inch) muffin cups with paper baking cups. Sift flour, baking soda, baking powder and salt into medium bowl. Combine sour cream, milk and vanilla in small bowl until well blended.

2. Beat granulated sugar and butter in large bowl with electric mixer at medium speed 2 minutes or until fluffy. Add eggs, 1 at a time, beating well after each addition. Add flour mixture alternately with sour cream mixture, beginning and ending with flour mixture, beating well after each addition. Stir in decors until blended. Spoon batter evenly into prepared muffin cups.

3. Bake 21 to 23 minutes or until toothpick inserted into centers comes out clean. Cool cupcakes in pan 5 minutes; remove to wire rack to cool completely

4. Stir food coloring into frosting in small bowl, a few drops at a time, until desired shade of pink is reached. Pipe or spread frosting on cupcakes. Arrange tiaras on cupcakes; sprinkle with sparkling sugars.

Makes 12 cupcakes

Pretty in Pink

Dragonflies

1 package (about 15 ounces) cake mix, any flavor, plus ingredients to prepare mix
White confectionery coating*
Pink, purple, yellow and green food coloring
44 small pretzel twists
22 pretzel sticks (about 3 inches)
1 container (16 ounces) vanilla frosting
White and purple nonpareils
Silver dragees

*Confectionery coating, also called almond bark or candy coating, can be found at craft stores and in the baking section of the supermarket. It comes in blocks, discs and chips and is usually available in white, milk and dark chocolate varieties.

1. Preheat oven to 350°F. Line 22 standard (2½-inch) muffin cups with paper baking cups.

2. Prepare cake mix according to package directions. Spoon batter into prepared muffin cups, filling two-thirds full. Bake 18 to 22 minutes or until toothpick inserted into centers comes out clean. Cool cupcakes in pans 10 minutes; remove to wire racks to cool completely.

3. Line large baking sheet with waxed paper. Melt confectionary coating according to package directions. Stir in pink food coloring, a few drops at a time, until desired shade of pink is reached. Dip pretzel twists in melted candy to coat; arrange 2 twists together on prepared baking sheet. Dip pretzel sticks in melted candy; place 1 stick between 2 pretzel twists to create dragonfly. Sprinkle pretzel twists with white nonpareils; arrange 2 purple nonpareils at top of pretzel sticks for eyes. Press dragees into bottom half of pretzel sticks. Let stand 10 minutes or until set.

4. Meanwhile, divide frosting between 3 small bowls. Add different food coloring (except pink) to each bowl, a few drops at a time, until desired shades are reached. Pipe or spread frosting on cupcakes; top with dragonflies.   *Makes 22 cupcakes*

Dragonflies

Just Plain Fun

Sunny Side Upcakes

1 package (about 15 ounces) vanilla cake mix, plus ingredients to prepare mix
22 yellow chewy fruit candies
2 containers (16 ounces each) vanilla frosting

1. Preheat oven to 350°F. Line 22 standard (2½-inch) muffin cups with paper baking cups.

2. Prepare cake mix according to package directions. Spoon batter into prepared muffin cups, filling two-thirds full. Bake 18 to 22 minutes or until toothpick inserted into centers comes out clean. Cool cupcakes in pans 10 minutes; remove to wire racks to cool completely.

3. For each egg yolk, microwave candy on LOW (30%) 5 seconds or just until softened. Shape into ball; flatten slightly.

4. Place 1 cup frosting in small microwavable bowl; microwave on LOW (30%) 10 seconds or until softened. Working with 1 cupcake at a time, spoon about 2 tablespoons frosting in center of cupcake. Spread frosting toward edges of cupcake in uneven petal shapes to resemble egg white. Press candy into frosting in center of cupcake. Microwave additional frosting as needed. *Makes 22 cupcakes*

Cookie in a Cupcake

1 package (16 ounces) refrigerated break-apart chocolate chip cookie dough (24 count), divided
2 cups all-purpose flour
$\frac{1}{2}$ cup unsweetened cocoa powder
1 teaspoon baking soda
$\frac{1}{2}$ teaspoon salt
$\frac{1}{2}$ cup (1 stick) butter, softened
1 cup sugar
1 egg
1 teaspoon vanilla
$\frac{1}{2}$ cup sour cream
$\frac{1}{2}$ cup hot water

1. Preheat oven to 350°F. Place 12 standard (2-inch) silicone muffin cups on large baking sheet or line 12 standard (2½-inch) muffin cups with paper baking cups.

2. Break apart half of cookie dough into 12 pieces along score lines. (Reserve remaining half of dough for another use.) Roll each piece of dough into a ball; refrigerate balls of dough while preparing cupcake batter.

3. Sift flour, cocoa, baking soda and salt into medium bowl. Beat butter in large bowl with electric mixer about 2 minutes or until creamy. Add sugar; beat 2 to 3 minutes or until light and fluffy. Beat in egg until well blended. Beat in vanilla.

4. Add sour cream and water to butter mixture alternately with flour mixture, beginning and ending with flour mixture. Beat until blended. Spoon batter evenly into prepared muffin cups. Place 1 ball of cookie dough into each cup, pressing down into batter.

5. Bake 20 to 22 minutes or until toothpick inserted into cake portion of cupcake comes out clean. Cool cupcakes in pan 5 minutes; remove to wire rack to cool slightly. Serve warm.

Makes 12 cupcakes

Cookie in a Cupcake

Hot Chocolate Cupcakes

1 package (about 16 ounces) pound cake mix, plus ingredients to prepare mix
4 containers (4 ounces each) prepared chocolate pudding*
2½ cups whipped topping, divided
4 small chewy chocolate candies
Unsweetened cocoa powder (optional)

*Or, purchase 1 (4-serving size) package instant chocolate pudding and pie filling mix and prepare according to package directions. Use 2 cups pudding for recipe; reserve remaining pudding for another use.

1. Preheat oven to 350°F. Spray 15 standard (2½-inch) muffin cups with baking spray (nonstick cooking spray with flour added) or grease and flour cups. Prepare cake mix according to package directions. Spoon batter into prepared muffin cups, filling about two-thirds full.

2. Bake 20 to 25 minutes or until toothpick inserted into centers comes out clean. Cool cupcakes in pans 5 minutes; remove to wire racks to cool completely.

3. Combine chocolate pudding and 2 cups whipped topping in medium bowl until well blended; refrigerate until ready to use.

4. Microwave chocolate candies on LOW (30%) 5 to 10 seconds or until slightly softened. Stretch each candy into long thin rope; cut ropes into 2-inch lengths. Curve candy pieces into "C" shape to resemble handles of mugs, pressing both ends of each handle to flatten slightly.

5. Cut out 2-inch circle about 1 inch deep from top of each cupcake with small paring knife. Cut 2 slits ½ inch apart in one side of each cupcake with small paring knife. Insert chocolate candy into slits to resemble mug handle. Fill hole in each cupcake with chocolate pudding mixture. Top with small dollop of remaining whipped topping; sprinkle with cocoa, if desired.

Makes 15 cupcakes

Hot Chocolate Cupcakes

Marshmallow Fudge Sundae Cupcakes

   1 package (about 15 ounces) chocolate cake mix, plus ingredients to prepare mix
   2 packages (4 ounces each) waffle bowls
40 large marshmallows
   1 jar (8 ounces) hot fudge topping
     Colored sprinkles or chopped nuts
1¼ cups whipped topping
   1 jar (10 ounces) maraschino cherries

1. Preheat oven to 350°F. Lightly spray 20 standard (2½-inch) muffin cups with nonstick cooking spray.

2. Prepare cake mix according to package directions. Spoon batter into prepared muffin cups, filling three-fourths full. Bake 20 to 22 minutes or until toothpick inserted into centers comes out clean. Cool cupcakes in pans 10 minutes; remove to wire racks to cool completely.

3. Place waffle bowls on ungreased baking sheets. Place one cupcake in each waffle bowl. Top each cupcake with 2 marshmallows; return to oven 2 minutes or until marshmallows are slightly softened.

4. Remove lid from hot fudge topping; microwave on HIGH 10 seconds or until softened. Top each cupcake with hot fudge topping, sprinkles, whipped topping and cherry.

Makes 20 cupcakes

Marshmallow Fudge Sundae Cupcakes

Quick Cookie Cupcakes

1 package (16 ounces) refrigerated break-apart chocolate chip cookie dough (24 count)
1½ cups chocolate frosting
Colored decors

1. Preheat oven to 350°F. Line 24 mini (1¾-inch) muffin cups with paper baking cups.

2. Break dough into 24 pieces along score lines. Roll each piece into a ball; place in prepared muffin cups. Bake 10 to 12 minutes or until golden brown. Cool cupcakes in pans 5 minutes; remove to wire racks to cool completely.

3. Pipe or spread frosting over each cupcake; sprinkle with decors.

Makes 24 mini cupcakes

Tip

These cupcakes are perfect for every occasion—they can be made in just minutes, and you can change the paper baking cups and decorations to match your theme. Use pink colors for Valentine's Day; green for St. Patrick's Day; red, white and blue for the 4th of July; and school colors for graduation parties. Craft stores usually stock baking cups and cake decorations in seasonal colors and patterns.

Quick Cookie Cupcakes

Cupcake Sliders

 2 cups all-purpose flour
2½ teaspoons baking powder
 ½ teaspoon salt
 1 cup milk
 ½ teaspoon vanilla
1½ cups sugar
 ½ cup (1 stick) butter, softened
 3 eggs
1¼ cups chocolate hazelnut spread or milk chocolate frosting

1. Preheat oven to 350°F. Spray 18 standard (2½-inch) muffin cups with nonstick cooking spray.

2. Combine flour, baking powder and salt in medium bowl. Combine milk and vanilla in measuring cup. Beat sugar and butter in large bowl with electric mixer at medium speed about 3 minutes or until creamy. Add eggs, 1 at a time, beating well after each addition. Add flour mixture alternately with milk mixture, ending with flour mixture, beating until well blended. Spoon batter into prepared muffin cups, filling three-fourths full.

3. Bake 18 to 20 minutes or until toothpick inserted into centers comes out clean. Cool cupcakes in pans 10 minutes; remove to wire racks to cool completely.

4. Cut off edges of cupcakes to form squares. Cut cupcakes in half crosswise. Spread each bottom half with about 1 tablespoon chocolate hazelnut spread; replace tops of cupcakes.

Makes 18 cupcakes

Cupcake Sliders

Crispy Cupcakes

¼ cup (½ stick) plus 2 tablespoons butter, divided
1 package (10½ ounces) marshmallows
½ cup creamy peanut butter
6 cups crisp rice cereal
1 cup bittersweet or semisweet chocolate chips
1½ cups powdered sugar
¼ cup milk

Microwave Directions

1. Spray 13×9-inch baking pan with nonstick cooking spray. Microwave 2 tablespoons butter in large microwavable bowl on HIGH 30 seconds or until melted. Add marshmallows; stir until coated with butter. Microwave on HIGH 1 minute; stir. Microwave 45 seconds; stir until melted. Stir in peanut butter until well blended. Add cereal; stir until blended.

2. Spread mixture in prepared pan, using waxed paper to spread and press into even layer. Let stand 10 to 15 minutes until set.

3. Meanwhile, place remaining ¼ cup butter and chocolate chips in medium microwavable bowl. Microwave on HIGH 40 seconds; stir. Microwave at additional 15-second intervals until melted and smooth. Gradually beat in powdered sugar and milk until well blended. Refrigerate frosting until ready to use.

4. Spray 1½-inch round cookie or biscuit cutter with nonstick cooking spray; cut out 36 circles from cereal bars. Place small dab of frosting on top of 18 circles; top with remaining 18 circles, pressing down firmly to seal. Place "cupcakes" in paper baking cups, if desired. Pipe or spread frosting on cupcakes. *Makes 18 cupcakes*

Crispy Cupcakes

Peanut Butter & Jelly Cupcakes

1 package (about 15 ounces) yellow cake mix, plus ingredients to prepare mix
¾ cup creamy peanut butter
½ cup (1 stick) butter, softened
2 cups powdered sugar
½ teaspoon vanilla
¼ cup milk
2 cups strawberry jelly

1. Preheat oven to 350°F. Line 22 standard (2½-inch) muffin cups with paper baking cups.

2. Prepare cake mix according to package directions. Spoon batter into prepared muffin cups, filling two-thirds full. Bake 18 to 22 minutes or until toothpick inserted into centers comes out clean. Cool cupcakes in pans 10 minutes; remove to wire racks to cool completely.

3. Beat peanut butter and butter in medium bowl with electric mixer at medium speed 2 minutes or until smooth. Add sugar and vanilla; beat at low speed 1 minute or until crumbly. Slowly add milk, beating at low speed until creamy.

4. Fill pastry bag fitted with small decorator tip with jelly. Insert tip into top of cupcake; squeeze bag gently to fill center of cupcake with jelly. (Stop squeezing when you feel resistance or jelly comes out of top of cupcake.) Repeat with remaining cupcakes and jelly.

5. Pipe or spread peanut butter frosting decoratively on cupcakes.   *Makes 22 cupcakes*

Peanut Butter & Jelly Cupcakes

Red Velvet Cupcakes

2¼ cups all-purpose flour
1 teaspoon salt
2 bottles (1 ounce each) red food coloring
3 tablespoons unsweetened cocoa powder
1 cup buttermilk
1 teaspoon vanilla
1½ cups sugar
½ cup (1 stick) butter, softened
2 eggs
1 teaspoon white vinegar
1 teaspoon baking soda
1 to 2 containers (16 ounces each) whipped cream cheese frosting
Toasted coconut* (optional)

To toast coconut, spread evenly on ungreased baking sheet. Bake in preheated 350°F oven 5 to 7 minutes or until light golden brown, stirring occasionally.

1. Preheat oven to 350°F. Line 18 standard (2½-inch) muffin cups with paper baking cups.

2. Combine flour and salt in medium bowl. Gradually stir food coloring into cocoa in small bowl until blended and smooth. Combine buttermilk and vanilla in separate bowl.

3. Beat sugar and butter in large bowl with electric mixer at medium speed about 4 minutes or until very light and fluffy. Add eggs, 1 at a time, beating well after each addition. Add cocoa mixture; beat until well blended and uniform in color. Add flour mixture alternately with buttermilk mixture, beating just until blended. Combine vinegar and baking soda in small bowl; gently fold into batter with spatula or spoon (do not use mixer). Spoon batter into prepared muffin cups, filling two-thirds full.

4. Bake 18 to 20 minutes or until toothpick inserted into centers comes out clean. Cool cupcakes in pans 10 minutes; remove to wire racks to cool completely.

5. Generously spread frosting over cupcakes. Sprinkle with coconut, if desired.

Makes 18 cupcakes

Red Velvet Cupcakes

Black & Whites

1 package (about 15 ounces) vanilla cake mix, plus ingredients to prepare mix
$^2/_3$ cup semisweet chocolate chips, melted
4 ounces cream cheese, softened
1 cup prepared vanilla frosting
1 cup prepared chocolate frosting

1. Preheat oven to 350°F. Line 22 standard (2½-inch) muffin cups with paper baking cups.

2. Prepare cake mix according to package directions. Reserve 2½ cups batter in medium bowl. Add melted chocolate and cream cheese to remaining batter; beat with electric mixer at medium speed about 2 minutes or until smooth and well blended.

3. Spoon chocolate and vanilla batters side by side into prepared muffin cups, filling about two-thirds full. (Use chocolate batter first as it is slightly thicker and easier to position on one side of muffin cups.)

4. Bake 16 to 18 minutes or until toothpick inserted into centers comes out clean. Cool cupcakes in pans 10 minutes; remove to wire racks to cool completely.

5. Spread vanilla frosting over half of each cupcake; spread chocolate frosting over remaining half of each cupcake.   *Makes 22 cupcakes*

Black & Whites

Mini Doughnut Cupcakes

   1 cup sugar
1½ teaspoons ground cinnamon
   1 package (about 15 ounces) yellow or white cake mix, plus ingredients to prepare mix
   1 tablespoon ground nutmeg

1. Preheat oven to 350°F. Grease and flour 48 mini (1¾-inch) muffin cups. Combine sugar and cinnamon in small bowl; set aside.

2. Prepare cake mix according to package directions; stir in nutmeg. Spoon batter into prepared muffin cups, filling two-thirds full.

3. Bake about 12 minutes or until lightly browned and toothpick inserted into centers comes out clean.

4. Remove cupcakes from pans. Roll warm cupcakes in sugar mixture until completely coated.   *Makes 48 mini cupcakes*

Note: These cupcakes are best served the day they are made.

Tip

Save any remaining cinnamon-sugar mixture to sprinkle on toast and pancakes.

Mini Doughnut Cupcakes

Peanut Butter & Milk Chocolate Cupcakes

1 package (about 15 ounces) butter recipe yellow cake mix with pudding in the mix, plus ingredients to prepare mix
½ cup creamy peanut butter
¼ cup (½ stick) butter, softened
2 bars (3½ ounces each) high-quality milk chocolate, broken into small pieces
¼ cup (½ stick) butter, cut into small chunks
¼ cup whipping cream
Dash salt
Peanut butter chips

1. Preheat oven to 350°F. Line 22 standard (2½-inch) muffin cups with paper baking cups.

2. Prepare cake mix according to package directions, using ½ cup peanut butter and ¼ cup softened butter instead of ½ cup butter called for in package directions. Spoon batter evenly into prepared muffin cups, filling two-thirds full.

3. Bake 24 to 26 minutes or until light golden brown and toothpick inserted into centers comes out clean. Cool cupcakes in pans 10 minutes; remove to wire racks to cool completely.

4. Combine chocolate, remaining ¼ cup butter, cream and salt in small, heavy saucepan. Heat over low heat, stirring constantly, just until butter and chocolate are melted. (Mixture should be warm, not hot.) Immediately spoon about 1 tablespoon chocolate glaze over each cupcake, spreading to cover top. Sprinkle with peanut butter chips.   *Makes 22 cupcakes*

Peanut Butter & Milk Chocolate Cupcakes

Party Pleasers

Strawberry Milkshake Cupcakes

2 cups all-purpose flour
1½ cups granulated sugar
4 teaspoons baking powder
½ teaspoon salt
1¼ cups (2½ sticks) butter, softened, divided
1 cup plus 6 to 8 tablespoons milk, divided
2 teaspoons vanilla, divided

3 eggs
2 containers (7 ounces each) plain Greek yogurt
1 cup seedless strawberry preserves
6 cups powdered sugar, divided
¼ cup shortening
Pink food coloring
Assorted pastel sugar pearls and decorating sugar

1. Preheat oven to 350°F. Line 24 standard (2½-inch) muffin cups with paper baking cups.

2. Beat flour, granulated sugar, baking powder and salt in large bowl with electric mixer at low speed until blended. Add ½ cup butter; beat at medium speed 30 seconds. Add 1 cup milk and 1 teaspoon vanilla; beat 2 minutes. Add eggs; beat 2 minutes. Spoon batter evenly into prepared muffin cups.

3. Bake 20 minutes or until toothpick inserted into centers comes out clean. Cool cupcakes in pans 10 minutes; remove to wire racks to cool completely.

4. For filling, combine yogurt and preserves in medium bowl. Transfer to piping bag fitted with medium round tip. Press tip into top of each cupcake and squeeze bag to fill.

5. Beat 3 cups powdered sugar, remaining ¾ cup butter, shortening, 4 tablespoons milk and remaining 1 teaspoon vanilla in large bowl with electric mixer at low speed until smooth. Add remaining 3 cups powdered sugar; beat until light and fluffy, adding remaining milk, 1 tablespoon at a time, as needed for desired consistency. Add food coloring, a few drops at a time, until desired shade of pink is reached. Pipe or spread frosting on cupcakes. Decorate as desired.

Makes 24 cupcakes

Honey Roasted Peanut Butter Minis

1¼ cups all-purpose flour
1 teaspoon baking powder
¼ teaspoon salt
⅔ cup packed brown sugar
½ cup creamy peanut butter
¼ cup vegetable oil
1 egg
2 tablespoons honey
½ cup milk
⅔ cup chopped honey roasted peanuts, divided
Honey Peanut Butter Frosting (recipe follows)

1. Preheat oven to 350°F. Line 28 mini (1¾-inch) muffin cups with paper baking cups.

2. Combine flour, baking powder and salt in small bowl. Combine brown sugar, peanut butter, oil, egg and honey in large bowl; stir until well blended and smooth. Add flour mixture and milk; mix just until combined. Stir in ⅓ cup chopped peanuts. Spoon batter evenly into prepared muffin cups.

3. Bake 15 minutes or until toothpick inserted into centers comes out clean. Cool cupcakes in pans 5 minutes; remove to wire racks to cool completely.

4. Prepare Honey Peanut Butter Frosting. Pipe or spread frosting on cupcakes; sprinkle with remaining ⅓ cup chopped peanuts. *Makes 28 mini cupcakes*

Honey Peanut Butter Frosting: Combine ⅔ cup creamy peanut butter, ¼ cup (½ stick) softened butter and ¼ cup honey in large bowl; stir until smooth. Stir in 1 cup powdered sugar until well blended.

Honey Roasted Peanut Butter Minis

Orange Dreamsicle Cupcakes

1½ cups all-purpose flour
1½ (0.15-ounce) envelopes orange unsweetened drink mix
2 teaspoons baking powder
⅛ teaspoon salt
1 cup granulated sugar
1 cup (2 sticks) butter, softened, divided
2 eggs
½ cup plus 3 tablespoons milk, divided
1½ teaspoons vanilla, divided
3 cups powdered sugar
Orange food coloring
White sprinkles

1. Preheat oven to 350°F. Line 12 standard (2½-inch) muffin cups with paper baking cups.

2. Whisk flour, drink mix, baking powder and salt in small bowl. Beat granulated sugar and ½ cup butter in medium bowl with electric mixer at medium speed until creamy. Add eggs, one at a time, beating well after each addition. Add flour mixture; beat until blended. Add ½ cup milk and 1 teaspoon vanilla; beat until smooth. Spoon batter evenly into prepared muffin cups.

3. Bake 20 minutes or until toothpick inserted into centers comes out clean. Cool cupcakes in pan 10 minutes; remove to wire rack to cool completely.

4. Beat powdered sugar, remaining ½ cup butter, 3 tablespoons milk and ½ teaspoon vanilla in large bowl with electric mixer at medium speed until fluffy. Add food coloring, a few drops at a time, until desired shade of orange is reached. Frost cupcakes; decorate with sprinkles.

Makes 12 cupcakes

Orange Dreamsicle Cupcakes

Crazy Colors Cupcakes

1 package (about 15 ounces) white cake mix
1 cup sour cream
3 eggs
½ cup vegetable oil
    Gel food coloring (4 colors)
1 container (16 ounces) white or cream cheese frosting
    Mini rainbow candy-coated chocolate chips

1. Preheat oven to 325°F. Line 20 standard (2½-inch) muffin cups with white paper baking cups.

2. Beat cake mix, sour cream, eggs and oil in large bowl with electric mixer at low speed 30 seconds. Beat at medium speed 2 minutes or until well blended. Divide batter evenly among four medium bowls; tint each bowl with different color food coloring. (Batter colors should be strong to retain color after baking.)

3. Spoon layer of one color batter into each prepared cup (about 2 teaspoons); spread batter to edge of cup with back of spoon or dampened fingers. Top with second color batter, making sure to completely cover first layer. Repeat with remaining two colors of batter. (If desired, switch order of colored layers halfway though assembly.)

4. Bake 18 to 20 minutes or until toothpick inserted into centers comes out clean. Cool cupcakes in pans 10 minutes; remove to wire racks to cool completely.

5. Frost cupcakes; decorate with rainbow chocolate chips.   *Makes 20 cupcakes*

Tips: Use as few or as many colors as you like for the rainbow layers and adjust the amount of batter in each cup accordingly. For faster layering of the different color batters, place each color batter into a disposable piping bag or plastic food storage bag with one corner cut off and pipe the layers into muffin cups instead of using a spoon.

Crazy Colors Cupcakes

Sailboat Cupcakes

11 chocolate peanut butter cups

16 squares white chocolate (2 [4-ounce] bars), divided

    Red, white and blue sprinkles or decors

 1 package (about 15 ounces) cake mix, any flavor, plus ingredients to prepare mix

 3 cups powdered sugar

⅓ cup boiling water

½ teaspoon vanilla

¼ teaspoon salt

 1 cup (2 sticks) butter, cut into pieces, softened

¼ cup shortening

    Blue food coloring

1. Cut peanut butter cups in half. Cut 11 white chocolate squares in half diagonally with sharp knife to create 22 triangles.

2. Place remaining 5 squares white chocolate in small microwavable bowl. Microwave on HIGH at 30-second intervals, stirring after each interval, until melted and smooth. Attach white chocolate sails to peanut butter cup boats using small amount of melted white chocolate. Lay sailboats on parchment paper 1 hour or until set. Decorate with sprinkles, using melted white chocolate to attach.

3. Preheat oven to 350°F. Line 22 standard (2½-inch) muffin cups with paper baking cups. Prepare and bake cupcakes according to package directions. Cool cupcakes in pans 5 minutes; remove to wire racks to cool completely.

4. Beat powdered sugar, boiling water, vanilla and salt in large bowl with electric mixer at low speed until smooth and cool. Add butter and shortening; beat at medium-high speed 3 minutes or until doubled in volume. Add food coloring, a few drops at a time, until desired shade of blue is reached.

5. Pipe frosting waves on cupcakes using piping bag fitted with star tip. Top cupcakes with sailboats.

Makes 22 cupcakes

Sailboat Cupcakes

Whoopie Pie Cupcakes

1 package (about 15 ounces) dark chocolate cake mix, plus ingredients to prepare mix
½ cup (1 stick) butter, softened
¼ cup shortening
3 cups powdered sugar
⅓ cup whipping cream
1 teaspoon salt

1. Preheat oven to 350°F. Grease 22 standard (2½-inch) muffin cups. Prepare cake mix according to package directions. Spoon batter into prepared muffin cups, filling two-thirds full.

2. Bake 20 minutes or until toothpick inserted into centers comes out clean. Cool cupcakes in pans 10 minutes; remove to wire racks to cool completely.

3. Beat butter and shortening in large bowl with electric mixer at medium speed until well blended. Add powdered sugar, cream and salt; beat at low speed 1 minute. Beat at medium-high speed 2 minutes or until fluffy.

4. Slice tops off cupcakes. Spread filling over bottoms of cupcakes; replace tops.

Makes 22 cupcakes

Whoopie Pie Cupcakes

Furry Monsters

Cupcakes

1½ cups all-purpose flour
1 teaspoon baking powder
½ teaspoon baking soda
½ teaspoon salt
½ cup (1 stick) butter, softened
1 cup granulated sugar
2 eggs
Grated peel and juice of 1 lemon
½ cup buttermilk

Frosting

2½ cups powdered sugar
Juice of 2 lemons
2 tablespoons boiling water
¼ teaspoon salt
¾ cup (1½ sticks) butter, cut into pieces, softened
Blue and green food coloring
Assorted candies and black string licorice
Black decorating gel

1. Preheat oven to 350°F. Line 12 standard (2½-inch) muffin cups with paper baking cups.

2. For cupcakes, combine flour, baking powder, baking soda and ½ teaspoon salt in medium bowl. Beat ½ cup butter and granulated sugar in large bowl with electric mixer at medium speed until creamy. Add eggs, peel and juice of 1 lemon; beat until well blended. Add flour mixture; beat at low speed while adding buttermilk. Beat just until combined. Spoon batter into prepared muffin cups, filling two-thirds full.

3. Bake 20 to 22 minutes or until toothpick inserted into centers comes out clean. Cool cupcakes in pan 5 minutes; remove to wire rack to cool completely.

4. For frosting, beat powdered sugar, juice of 2 lemons, boiling water and ¼ teaspoon salt in large bowl with electric mixer at low speed until smooth and cool. Add ¾ cup butter; beat at medium-high speed 3 minutes or until doubled in volume. Divide frosting between two bowls; add food coloring, a few drops at a time, until desired shades are reached.

5. Pipe fur on cupcakes using piping bag fitted with star tip. Decorate cupcakes with candies and licorice to create monster faces. Pipe dot of decorating gel in each eye.

Makes 12 cupcakes

Cupcake Teepees

1 package (9 ounces) yellow cake mix, plus ingredients to prepare mix
1 jar (7½ ounces) marshmallow creme
24 fruit rollups

1. Preheat oven to 350°F. Spray 40 mini (1¾-inch) muffin cups with nonstick cooking spray. Prepare cake mix according to package directions. Spoon batter into prepared muffin cups, filling half full.

2. Bake 12 minutes or until toothpick inserted into centers comes out clean. Cool cupcakes in pans 5 minutes; remove to wire racks to cool completely.

3. Turn cupcakes upside down on large serving platter. Spoon 1 tablespoon marshmallow creme on top of each cupcake.

4. Unwrap and unroll fruit rollups; lay flat on work surface. Cut 20 circles from fruit rollups using 4-inch stiff paper or cardboard circle as template. Cut each circle in half.

5. To form teepee, place center of round side of one half-circle at bottom of one cupcake; wrap ends around cupcake. Repeat with remaining fruit rollups and cupcakes. Serve immediately.   *Makes 40 mini cupcakes*

Variation: Experiment with different flavors of cake, fruit rollups and fillings. For a strawberry shortcake flavor, use white cake mix, whipped cream instead of marshmallow creme and strawberry-flavored fruit rollups.

Cupcake Teepees

Blue Suede Cupcakes

2¼ cups all-purpose flour
1 teaspoon salt
2 bottles (1 ounce each) blue food coloring
3 tablespoons unsweetened cocoa powder
1 cup buttermilk
1 teaspoon vanilla
1½ cups granulated sugar
1 cup (2 sticks) butter, softened, divided
2 eggs
1 teaspoon white vinegar
1 teaspoon baking soda
1 package (8 ounces) cream cheese, softened
3 cups powdered sugar
2 tablespoons milk
Additional blue food coloring
Blue decorating sugar

1. Preheat oven to 350°F. Line 20 standard (2½-inch) muffin cups with paper baking cups.

2. Whisk flour and salt in medium bowl. Gradually stir food coloring into cocoa in small bowl until blended and smooth. Combine buttermilk and vanilla in another small bowl.

3. Beat granulated sugar and ½ cup butter in large bowl with electric mixer at medium speed 4 minutes or until light and fluffy. Add eggs, one at a time, beating well after each addition. Add cocoa mixture; beat until well blended. Add flour mixture alternately with buttermilk mixture, beating just until blended. Stir vinegar into baking soda in small bowl; gently fold into batter (do not use mixer). Spoon batter evenly into prepared muffin cups.

4. Bake 20 minutes or until toothpick inserted into centers comes out clean. Cool cupcakes in pans 10 minutes; remove to wire racks to cool completely.

5. Beat remaining ½ cup butter and cream cheese in large bowl with electric mixer at medium-high speed until smooth. Gradually beat in powdered sugar at low speed. Beat in milk until blended. Add additional food coloring, a few drops at a time, until desired shade of blue is reached. Frost cupcakes; sprinkle with decorating sugar. *Makes 20 cupcakes*

Blue Suede Cupcakes

Triple Scoop Cupcakes

1 cup all-purpose flour
¾ cup sugar
2 teaspoons baking powder
¼ teaspoon salt
¼ cup (½ stick) butter, softened
⅓ cup milk
½ teaspoon vanilla
2 eggs
½ (16-ounce) container white or cream cheese frosting
Butter waffle cookies
Pastel-colored thin candy wafers
Jumbo confetti sprinkles

1. Preheat oven to 350°F. Line 12 standard (2½-inch) muffin cups with paper baking cups.

2. Beat flour, sugar, baking powder and salt in large bowl with electric mixer at low speed until blended. Add butter; beat at medium speed 30 seconds. Add milk and vanilla; beat 2 minutes. Add eggs; beat 2 minutes. Spoon batter evenly into prepared muffin cups.

3. Bake 20 minutes or until toothpick inserted into centers comes out clean. Cool cupcakes in pan 10 minutes; remove to wire rack to cool completely.

4. Frost cupcakes. Use paring knife to cut 1½-inch-long triangles from butter cookies to resemble ice cream cones. Place one triangle on each cupcake; top with three candy wafers. Decorate edges of cupcakes with sprinkles.

Makes 12 cupcakes

Triple Scoop Cupcakes

·Index·

VOLUME MEASUREMENTS (dry)

$^1/_8$ teaspoon = 0.5 mL
$^1/_4$ teaspoon = 1 mL
$^1/_2$ teaspoon = 2 mL
$^3/_4$ teaspoon = 4 mL
1 teaspoon = 5 mL
1 tablespoon = 15 mL
2 tablespoons = 30 mL
$^1/_4$ cup = 60 mL
$^1/_3$ cup = 75 mL
$^1/_2$ cup = 125 mL
$^2/_3$ cup = 150 mL
$^3/_4$ cup = 175 mL
1 cup = 250 mL
2 cups = 1 pint = 500 mL
3 cups = 750 mL
4 cups = 1 quart = 1 L

VOLUME MEASUREMENTS (fluid)

1 fluid ounce (2 tablespoons) = 30 mL
4 fluid ounces ($^1/_2$ cup) = 125 mL
8 fluid ounces (1 cup) = 250 mL
12 fluid ounces (1$^1/_2$ cups) = 375 mL
16 fluid ounces (2 cups) = 500 mL

WEIGHTS (mass)

$^1/_2$ ounce = 15 g
1 ounce = 30 g
3 ounces = 90 g
4 ounces = 120 g
8 ounces = 225 g
10 ounces = 285 g
12 ounces = 360 g
16 ounces = 1 pound = 450 g

DIMENSIONS

$^1/_{16}$ inch = 2 mm
$^1/_8$ inch = 3 mm
$^1/_4$ inch = 6 mm
$^1/_2$ inch = 1.5 cm
$^3/_4$ inch = 2 cm
1 inch = 2.5 cm

OVEN TEMPERATURES

250°F = 120°C
275°F = 140°C
300°F = 150°C
325°F = 160°C
350°F = 180°C
375°F = 190°C
400°F = 200°C
425°F = 220°C
450°F = 230°C

BAKING PAN SIZES

Utensil	Size in Inches/Quarts	Metric Volume	Size in Centimeters
Baking or Cake Pan (square or rectangular)	8×8×2	2 L	20×20×5
	9×9×2	2.5 L	23×23×5
	12×8×2	3 L	30×20×5
	13×9×2	3.5 L	33×23×5
Loaf Pan	8×4×3	1.5 L	20×10×7
	9×5×3	2 L	23×13×7
Round Layer Cake Pan	8×1½	1.2 L	20×4
	9×1½	1.5 L	23×4
Pie Plate	8×1¼	750 mL	20×3
	9×1¼	1 L	23×3
Baking Dish or Casserole	1 quart	1 L	—
	1½ quart	1.5 L	—
	2 quart	2 L	—

·Metric Conversion Chart·